Caught in the Act of Grace

A Sexual Abuse Recovery Bible Study for Women

CAUGHT IN THE ACT OF GRACE: A SEXUAL ABUSE RECOVERY

BIBLE STUDY FOR WOMEN

© Copyright 2010 by Darla Weaver

Book cover design is by Michelle Williams at treasuredpages.com.

Printed in the United States of America

For More Information:
Acts of Grace Ministries
PO Box 1409
Montgomery, Texas 77356

ISBN #: 978-0-9831654-0-8

Special Thanks

I would like to give a special thanks to my husband and children for the patience and love that you have given me over all of these years. You are my heart and life. I would never have tried to begin this ministry without your support and understanding. Thank you for always being proud of me.

Thank you to my friends who have surrounded me with your wisdom, knowledge, willingness to roll up your sleeves and dive in with me, who pushed me when I needed to be pushed and made me stop when I needed to stop. Especially Kim Stokes, you never left me alone when I was in some of my most lonely hours of healing. To Vicki Parker who helped me understand the last part of my need to forgive my abusers and to all the women who helped pray me through that journey. To Sydna Masse, who told me over and over and over that I could and *should* do this ministry.

My most special thanks are to my best friend, God. You are the rock that I stand on. You have never left me, neither have You forsaken me. You have shown me that I am more than I knew. You have shown me that my secrets were not my own, but they are meant to help people, and were always safe with You.

This book is dedicated in loving memory of Betty Oliver, the one person who told me I could not only write, but helped me do it until it was no longer possible for her. I long for the day that I can see her smiling face again.

Broken Dreams

*As children bring their broken toys
with tears for us to mend,
I brought my broken dreams to God
because He was my Friend.
But then instead of leaving Him
in peace to work alone,
I hung around and tried to help
with ways that were my own.
At last I snatched them back and cried,
"How can You be so slow" -
"My child," He said,
"What could I do? You never did let go. "*

-Author Unknown-

Table of Contents

How to Use Caught in the Act of Grace Bible Study for Women

1.) Caught in the Act of Grace can be used by an individual for personal study, but the recommendation is for use in a small group setting.

2.) In a small group setting it is recommended for no more than five and no fewer than two people in a group with a leader and co-leader.

3.) The leader and co-leader should each have a "Caught in the Act of Grace Leader's Guide" which includes instructions and exercises each week that complements each chapter in the Bible Study book. The Bible Study leaders should have also completed the Acts of Grace Bible Study Training at one of our Leadership Conferences.

4.) Do a small amount of each chapter every day. The daily work will help you to absorb the information instead of rushing through it. Whatever work you put into the Bible study determines the results you will receive.

5.) Use a journal daily as part of this study to write any thoughts, prayers or letters to people to whom you would like to say something but may not have the ability to do so. Make sure that you are honest about your feelings and that the words written are exactly what you want to say. Your journal is for you only. Make sure that you do not leave it in any public location in your home, car or work. Explain to the members of your household that this journal is for your healing, and their respect for your privacy will not only protect them from too much information, but also is important to allow you to safely and privately journey through your past.

For more information, please visit our website at www.actsofgrace.net.

Acts of Grace Ministries

Our Mission

Reaching a wounded world through the tender love of Christ.

Our Vision

- To Disciple and help people develop a closer and more fulfilling relationship with God, their family, peers, church and themselves. (John 3:16)

- To Establish a purpose plan for life, therefore bringing true contentment to themselves through helping others and reconnecting. (Jer. 29:11)

- To Teach people to play on purpose and reconnect with our peers, because we need each other.

- To Teach strategies to overcome the urge to run away when life overwhelms them by being a steadfast and constant reminder of the unconditional love of Christ.

- To Walk out the journey of life from physical or social isolation to socialization with Christ and His church.

We Believe

- All life has value and should be treated with dignity and honor.

- Every life has purpose and each individual should be given the chance to make a difference in our world.

- Forgiveness is not an option but it is a mandate from God for the health and well-being of human heart.

- Jesus Christ is the only hope for our family, church, community, nation and the world, and through Him, we can do all things.

- Grace and mercy can be obtained, by a willing heart and for a willing heart.

How to Invite Jesus Christ Into Your
Heart as Your Personal Savior?

As you work through this Bible study you will come to places that seem too difficult for you to deal with. You would be correct in that feeling. In and of yourself you cannot find the peace that comes through the grace and mercy of God. Because of this we believe that all healing and change in our lives comes from accepting Jesus Christ as Lord and Savior. Becoming a Christian is not something that you do once a week attending church or carrying a Bible in your car. It is who you become. Christianity creates a change in desires, things you want to do, places you want to go, and how you function in your day to day life. As you read and study your Bible you will begin to learn how God wants you to live. A new joy will take over the old habits that have torn your life apart. God created you with great things in mind for your well-being. He loves you as much as He loves Jesus, His only son. You are uniquely and wonderfully made as a vital part of this world at this time in history. You cannot be substituted nor can you be recreated. You are necessary and needed. If you have never accepted Jesus into your heart, please read the following verses.

"I am the way, the truth, and the life!" Jesus answered. "*Without me, no one can go to the Father."* John 14:6 (NKJV)

Good works cannot save you.

"*You were saved by faith in God, who treats us much better than we deserve. This is God's gift to you, and not anything you have done on your own. It isn't something you have earned, so there is nothing you can brag about.*" Ephesians 2:8-9 (NKJV)

Trust Jesus Christ today! Here's what you must do:

1st: Admit you are a sinner.

"*All of us have sinned and fallen short of God's glory.*" Romans 3:23 (NKJV)

"*Adam sinned, and that sin brought death into the world. Now everyone has sinned, and so everyone must die.*" Romans 5:12 (NKJV)

"*If we say that we have not sinned, we make God a liar, and his message isn't in our hearts.*" 1 John 1:10 (NKJV)

2nd: Be willing to turn from sin (repent).

"*Not at all! But you can be sure that if you don't turn back to God, every one of you will also die.*" Luke 13:5 (NKJV)

"*In the past, God forgave all this because people did not know what they were doing. But now he says that everyone everywhere must turn to him.*" Acts 17:30 (NKJV)

3rd: Believe that Jesus Christ died for you, was buried, and rose from the dead.

"*God loved the people of this world so much that he gave his only Son, so that everyone who has faith in him will have eternal life and never really die.*" John 3:16 (NKJV)

"*But God showed how much he loved us by having Christ die for us, even though we were sinful.*" Romans 5:8 (NKJV)

"*So you will be saved, if you honestly say, "Jesus is Lord," and if you believe with all your heart that God raised him from death.*" Romans 10:9 (NKJV)

4th: Through prayer, invite Jesus into your life to become your personal Savior.

"*God will accept you and save you, if you truly believe this and tell it to others.*" Romans 10:10 (NKJV)

"*All who call out to the Lord will be saved.*" Romans 10:13 (NKJV)

If you believe what you read is true then pray: Dear God, please forgive me of my past and my sin. I believe that You sent your Son Jesus Christ to shed His precious blood and die for me. I ask that You help me to stop doing things that hurt You and me. I thank You Jesus, for coming into my heart and my life and for being my personal Savior.

Now what do you do:

Read your Bible every day to get to know Christ better.

> "*Do your best to win God's approval as a worker who doesn't need to be ashamed and who teaches only the true message.*" 2 Timothy 2:15 (NKJV)

> "*Your word is a lamp that gives light wherever I walk.*" Psalm 119:105 (NKJV)

Talk to God in prayer every day.

> "*If you have faith when you pray, you will be given whatever you ask for.*" Matthew 21:22 (NKJV)

> "*Don't worry about anything, but pray about everything. With thankful hearts offer up your prayers and requests to God.*" Philippians 4:6 (NKJV)

Be baptized, worship, fellowship, and serve with other Christians in a church where Christ is preached and the Bible is the final authority.

> "*Go to the people of all nations and make them my disciples. Baptize them in the name of the Father, the Son, and the Holy Spirit.*" Matthew 28:19 (NKJV)

"Some people have gotten out of the habit of meeting for worship, but we must not do that. We should keep on encouraging each other, especially since you know that the day of the Lord's coming is getting closer." Hebrews 10:25 (NKJV)

"Everything in the Scriptures is God's Word. All of it is useful for teaching and helping people and for correcting them and showing them how to live." 2 Timothy 3:16 (NKJV)

Tell others about Christ.

"Then he told them: Go and preach the good news to everyone in the world." Mark 16:15 (NKJV)

"I don't have any reason to brag about preaching the good news. Preaching is something God told me to do, and if I don't do it, I am doomed." 1 Corinthians 9:16 (NKJV)

"I am proud of the good news! It is God's powerful way of saving all people who have faith, whether they are Jews or Gentiles." Romans 1:16 (NKJV)

Chapter 1

Where Do I Start?

Objective:

- Identify where I have been and where I am going.

- Define sexual abuse and identify the task areas of healing.

- Recognize some of the secondary symptoms of sexual abuse.

- Illustrate my personal definition of sexual abuse through words or drawings – (Begin to face my giants through words or drawings).

Inspiration:

> *A Prayer of the Afflicted; When he is overwhelmed and faint and pours out his complaint to God. "1)HEAR MY prayer, 0 Lord, and let my cry come to You. 2) Hide not your face from me in the day when I am in distress! Incline Your ear to me; in the day when I call, answer me speedily. 3) For my days consume away like smoke, and my bones burn like a firebrand or like a hearth. 4) My heart is smitten like grass and withered, so that [in absorption] I forget to eat my food. 5) By reason of my loud groaning [from suffering and trouble] my flesh cleaves to my bones. 6) I am like a melancholy pelican or vulture of the wilderness; I am like a [desolate] owl of the waste places. 7) I am sleepless and lie awake [mourning], like a bereaved sparrow alone on the housetop. Psalm 102:1–7 (Amplified)*

The Journey Begins...

The writer of Psalm 102, King David, gives a very descriptive and accurate speech about how he is feeling at a moment in time when he has nowhere else to go with this pain except to God. Often, in an attempt to understand our lives, we analyze our circumstances to the point of insanity, leaving us in a pit of sadness and overwhelming immobility. At times, the future seems as foreboding as the past, but with every tick of the clock, our future continues to march forward with us unwillingly swept away in its current. The passing of time should never cause anyone distress as long as they know how to swim safely with the currents of life. However, for those who have been taken places they did not choose to go in their emotions, mentally and physically, the currents of life can feel more like a deadly undertow both physically and mentally. What lies ahead for some is an unknown void into a black pit of uncertainty and fear, instead of anticipation of life filled with joy and fulfilling relationships.

The breakthrough now is only a step away. Up until now, because of your circumstances, the step you have avoided for all of this time is exposure. Refusal to look at the past in a healthy way will only leave the memories of the past exactly where they have always been in your daily juggling act of pretense. Simply admitting that sexual abuse really did occur in your life falls somewhere between overwhelming and relief. But where you go from here is up to you.

In making this change in your life, you are willingly moving into a new area of healing. Your newfound attitude of courage is not dependent on "fixing" your past, "getting over it so I can forget it" attitude, or unrealistic change. Your newfound bravery is simply a desire to face what has happened to you so that you no longer have to wonder if the way you feel about yourself is different from how others feel about themselves. "I thought I act the way I do because it was just my personality" is a comment that is repeated often. Perhaps now is the time to realize you are normal for someone who has been through the abuse that you have been through -- you are not strange or a freak.

As you begin to stop fighting memories of your abuse as they trickle into your mind, the discomfort factor may overpower the ability to focus on and deal with those memories. But, if you allow each piece of the past to come to you one at a time, then each piece can be digested and dealt with in a proper way. Remember, God will never allow you to remember more than you need for recovery.

℠

Just as an onion has many layers, we have layers of things from our past that may need to be "dealt with."

To cut into an onion all at one time can bring tears and a painful experience. But to take it apart one layer at a time is a much more tolerable experience.

We will look at one layer at this time ~ sexual abuse.

℠

To force memories will only cause frustration and more denial. Forcing of memories can also lead to making up events that never occurred. Memories can come in different forms such as sounds, sights, events, smells, or a person who may resemble your abuser. Flashbacks or triggers can bring up events that cause bodily reactions.

What Sexual Abuse Is

According to Dr. Dan Allender, sexual abuse is "any contact or interaction (visual, verbal, or suggestive) between two people (this could be either a child, adolescent, or adult), where one of the persons is being used for the sexual stimulation of the other person (perpetrator or secondary person)."[1]

Task Areas of Healing	**Secondary Symptoms**
• Facing the abuse	• Low self esteem
• Shame	• Depression
• Betrayal	• Addictive behaviors and abuse
• Powerlessness	• Sexual dysfunction
• Contempt of others or self	• Eating disorders
• Ambivalence	• Physical complaints
• Unforgiveness of others, self and God	• Self destructive behaviors

Sexual Abuse Wound

Use the space below to draw a picture of what your sexual abuse wound looks like to you. You may use words to describe your wound

Use the next two pages to *JOURNAL* what you can remember of your sexual abuse. Remember not to force memories. Rather, allow yourself to remember only what God wants you to remember.

1.) At this point, stop and ask God if there is anything more that you remember that you did not previously write down.

2.) Have you ever talked to anyone to confirm your memories? If so, whom did you speak to and what did they tell you?

In relationships with the people close to you, there may have been times when your reactions to circumstances were obviously more than necessary. For example, your husband asked you to get him a glass of water and your response was, "Go get it yourself. I am not your maid or your slave."

The way we relate to people is a direct result of the way we were raised and the events in our lives that shaped our belief system. Whether these are positive or negative, our belief systems are a driving force in our relational style or how we treat people. It is also how we think of ourselves. Because you cannot give away what you do not have, love and respect for yourself is key to giving love and respect to others. If you are filled with a negative self-image, you will give a negative image of yourself to everyone you come in contact with. For most of us, the way we relate in normal everyday activities can be calm and happy. But the moment something stressful is added, we feel pressure come inside of us, and the need to protect ourselves by whatever means necessary propels our relational ability into something resembling Dr. Jekyll turning into Mr. Hyde. This protection reaction is rarely a thought through and planned response. It is a fight or flight reaction put in us by a loving God to help protect ourselves from a real threat in the present. Our heightened state of self-protection becomes our new normal and a hair pin trigger is our lifestyle.

3.) When pressure events happen, what response do you have to them -- fight or flight?

4.) What are your actions in this response? Do you wound yourself or others with words or behavior? Remember, passive aggression (flight) can be more hurtful than aggressive aggression (fight).

5.) What is one thing that you find the most hurtful in how others treat you?

6.) When you strike out at someone or they have struck out at you, can you stop and realize the original source of the wound? For example, you are fighting with your child about how little she helps around the house when she is the cause of most of the mess. But the real reason you are angry with her is that she did not put your favorite shirt back after she borrowed it like she said she would. Name and explain a time when you have allowed yourself to do this.

7.) The Bible says that Satan goes around like a roaring lion, seeking whom he may devour. Can you write about a time when you have felt like you verbally "devoured" someone in your anger toward them?

8.) When we treat someone in a way that the Bible calls a sin, we are behaving toward that person in the same way that we were treated by our abuser. Control was taken away from us by the abuser, so now we will "never be controlled again." In an effort to never be controlled, we become controlling. Name a situation where you controlled someone by your actions or words. How did it make you feel at the time?

9.) Are you able to see yourself in a new way with the relationships that you are involved in currently? If so, how?

10.) Describe how you would like to treat others and be treated by others.

11.) Check off as many of the following statements that may apply to you:

___ I don't understand why I act the way that I do.

___ I don't understand why I keep getting into bad/unfulfilling/inappropriate relationships.

___ I feel that if I were not so ____________________, this would have never happened.

___ I often wonder why no one seems to like me.

___ I am so lonely and everyone else has friends.

___ I would rather be alone and do my own thing; people are a pain.

___ I don't care.

___ This is all my fault. It is always my fault.

___ I am such a bad person; no wonder no one likes me.

___ If I had just not said anything, then they would not be mad at me.

___ If I keep being ____________, no one will know the real me.

___ I hope no one ever finds out about ____________ because if they knew who I really am on the inside, they would hate me.

We all have our catch phrases to describe ourselves and how we feel. When we speak positive words about ourselves, then a positive self-image emerges. But when negative words are spoken, we continually tear down the very spirit inside ourselves that gives us life and joy. The renewing of the thinking process about ourselves is key to how others will relate to us in return. Allowing ourselves to be vulnerable is not a weakness but a strength. It takes more determination to not run or fight than it does to stand and face the battle raging inside of us.

The Master of Healing

By Darla Weaver

My father-in-law once owned a young filly that he had raised from one of his brood mares. She was a flashy little paint, with a mischievous and rowdy edge. She never went anywhere that was not at a dead run with a little bucking mixed in. When it was time to wean her from the mare, he put her into a pen that was made of fence panels attached to metal T posts. The day came when, at feeding time, she stood in the middle of the pen wounded. She had run into the fence, ran a T post into her shoulder and tore herself open all the way to the bone and from front to back. She looked as if someone had tried to cut her right leg off her body, but had decided to quit halfway through instead.

My father-in-law quickly loaded her in the trailer and took her to the veterinarian. The vet cleaned the wound and stitched her back together. She received shots for infections, supplies for continued medication, and was then sent home to recuperate. Having raised horses his entire life, my father-in-law knew how to take care of this uncooperative little filly, but a problem still developed. On the outside, the filly looked like she was healing and getting better. But on the inside, she was a raging mess. Deep inside the wound, under the stitches where the medication could not reach, an infection had begun in spite of everyone's best efforts. Once the infection began, it soon spread.

The filly's eyes were the only sign of something wrong at first, but then she began to limp more than before and soon she stopped eating. All efforts to heal the filly seemed to be in vain. Though the veterinarian had done a good job of making neat stitches on the outside, they would have to be removed. The wound had to be opened and exposed or she would die.

Once opened, the wound exposed an infection-filled mass of oozing pus. The pus was an invitation for more infection, and for flies to hatch their eggs. But the master was there and he would not allow that to happen.

Two, sometimes three times a day, my father-in-law would cleanse the filly's wound with water, then spread salve on it, and lastly, spray it with fly spray. Symbolically, the water washed away the past few hours of built-up infection, just as our daily devotions wash us with the water of the Word (Ephesians 5:26). The salve filled the wound with healing ointment, just as our faith and belief in Jesus fills and heals our deepest wounds with the Balm of Gilead, comforting us and bringing us peace, for He is the Great Physician (Jer. 8:22, Mark 2:17, John 9:6). The fly spray provided a barrier between the wound and the things in the filly's environment that could cause more infection. God provides this same barrier for our wounds by being our Shield and Deliverer. (Psalm 18:2).

                                     Caught in the Act of Grace Women's Bible Study

All of these healing elements would have never have been given to the filly if not for her master. On her own, the filly stood, wounded, infected, dying; it was the master who came to her with love, gentleness, and knowledge of what was needed to heal such a gaping, nasty mess in her life.

Ironically, each time he went to her to help her, the filly would resist. It hurt to have the wound touched and medicated. She fought him so much that sometimes my father-in-law had to tie her tight to a snubbing post, just to make her stand still and accept the help that she needed. During the treatment, and then again, afterwards, he always spoke soothing words to her, stroking her calmly, and helping her to not be frightened. At first, the fight was not so hard for my father-in-law to deal with -- the filly hurt too much to make a fuss. But when the wound began to get a little better and the filly felt some relief from the original pain, her strength returned. The old fight rose back up inside her and she began to resent what he was doing for her.

With a lot of patience and a consistent refusal to back away and let her live with herself, my father-in-law allowed the filly's wound to heal in the proper way -- from the inside out. It took time, care, willingness to sacrifice his own needs and desires, and mercy and grace to forgive the filly's rebellion towards him. But mostly it took love. Eventually, the wound healed, the filly became a mare, and the mare became one of my father-in-law's most cherished possessions. As a symbol of healing and the faithfulness of the master to help his own, a scar remains on her shoulder, but you have to know where to find it.

At the time of the accident, I named the filly Frankenstein because she looked like someone tried to put her leg back on her body. Later, her name was shortened to Frankie. Eventually, her nicknamed disappeared. Now, the filly is whole, complete, well, and the past is merely a scar with a memory.

That is what God wants to do for us. He wants to be the Master of our healing. He wants the healing to be complete. Nevertheless, in order to have healing, we must allow God to open up the wound, cleanse it daily, and fill it with the only medication that heals - His love. The tenderness that we experience in the healing process can be excruciating and necessary. God will never be the Master who snubs you to a snubbing post to make you stand still and take what you need to be whole and healthy. God is the Master who is willing to wait until you finish bucking, biting and complaining each day as He comes to you wherever you are. He will heal you from the inside out. It is our decision so let's move forward and not allow the pus of life to infect every area of our being.

Dear God,

In Jesus' Name, Amen.

REMINDER: Please remember to Journal daily …

[1] *The Wounded Heart: Hope for Adult Victims of Childhood Sexual Abuse*" pg. 48, by Dr. Dan Allender, Nav Press, Revised Edition (May 1, 1990)

Chapter 2

How Could
This Happen To Me?

Objective:

- Discover the spiritual component of sexual abuse recovery.
- How does sexual abuse happen?
- Learn that history does repeat itself.

Inspiration:

> *Job 23:2-6 (AMP) 2) Even today is my complaint rebellious and bitter; my stroke is heavier than my groaning. 3) Oh, that I knew where I might find Him, that I might come even to His seat! 4) I would lay my cause before Him and fill my mouth with arguments. 5) I would learn what He would answer me, and understand what He would say to me. 6) Would He plead against me with His great power? No, He would give heed to me. [Isa. 27:4, 5; 57:16.]*

The Journey Continues…

Remembering the sexual abuse of the past is an experience avoided at all cost for many survivors. Memories surrounding the abuse can be overpowering in a manner not experienced other times in life. The fear of exposure is stifling at best. More often exposure is the cause of panic and self-protection. Why do victims feel responsible in some way for the abuse that has been done to them? Was there something about them that was perverted, so it attracted a pervert? Was there something bad about them that caused them to deserve being abused? Was the timing and place so predetermined that they could not avoid the abuser?

In order to come to terms with the past, we must know the past. Our memories tell us we already have an acquaintance with abuse we would like to shed from ourselves. Triggers and flashbacks pop into our memory at the most inopportune times. Pressure from certain types of people sends us into panic or rages that, at times, feel like out of body experiences. Why is this? The past is always going to be a part of the present until we deal with the pain caused by it. In dealing with the past, there must be honesty in the feelings associated with the abuse. The family structure we remember must be revisited in order to understand the roles of the entire family at that particular time. The fear of feeling must be overcome for it is our feelings that are wounded and where we must be healed.

The Spiritual Component of Sexual Abuse Recovery

Many times in my life I have felt as though the situation I am in warrants God taking me home so I can avoid dealing with my lack of desire to cope through the hard times. I don't want to rise above my pain. I don't want to let the other person off the hook. I don't want to be the first to forgive. I don't want to do anything but be mad. There is no place in the Bible that says I can do anything but the opposite of what my humanness demands. Rising above, forgiving first, getting over my anger is what I should do; but something inside of me, deep inside, will not allow me to do "the right thing" with ease. What is the wall I keep running up against in my mind?

When looking back at the past there can be a desire to run, not always physically but mentally. We choose to NOT deal with our hurts, but to pretend like they are not there. If someone in our lives begins to pressure us, moving us in the direction of healing, we feel as though death is knocking at our door. Conversations then resemble a game of tag. Whoever is "it" chases us verbally, ducking and diving around trees of memories, hiding behind cars that block our vision of the chaser, straining our every attempt to not be caught so that we will become "it", making all eyes focus upon us and our wounds.

The first line of Psalm 23:4 (NKJV) "*Yea, though I walk through the valley of the shadow of death*" negates our excuse to run away. At times we feel as though we are dying as we walk through a valley that feels like death. The second half of the verse, "*I will fear no evil: for Thou art with me; thy rod and thy staff they comfort me*" is never even considered. We are unable to get past the valley of death in our thoughts to understand that there is no evil to fear because God is with us to guide and protect us in a manner bringing great comfort. This comfort He offers is beyond our human ability to understand and yet it is the very comfort we need in order to be healed of our wounds.

We wonder -- if the very protection and guidance we deserved before we were abused was lacking from our earthly protectors, how can we trust God to protect and guide us? As Christians, we do not dare speak doubt that God might not protect us from being abused. It would mean there is a lack of faith or a flaw in our faith, and we potentially will be firmly rebuked for that lack. But where was God when the abuse was occurring? Why did He not stop the abuse? If we are to fear no evil, why are we allowed to experience it in such a painful manner?

Revelation 21:4 (AMP) "God will wipe away every tear from their eyes; and death shall be no more, neither shall there be anguish (sorrow and mourning) nor grief nor pain any more, for the old conditions and the former order of things have passed away." [Isaiah 25:8; 35:10.]

How Does Sexual Abuse Happen?

Over the years, I have studied the causes of abuse such as how the abuser selects the victim, what the abuser is like mentally, and how a victim can overcome all of the damage. The stages of abuse having the clearest meanings for me are what will be used to help answer seemingly unanswerable questions.

The stages of sexual abuse are:

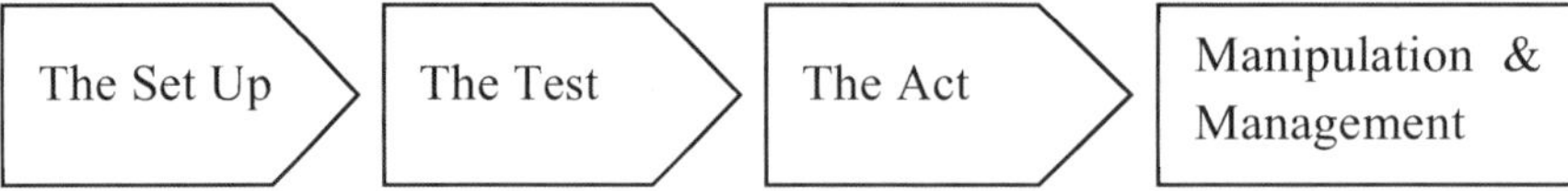

At the end of each stage are questions designed to lead you through that stage, whether your sexual abuse was molestation, rape, prostitution, or perhaps consensual in return for something like a place to live, attention, a promotion or even a grade in school. Do not skip any of the questions because almost all fit any form of sexual abuse.

Below is a fictitious story that details the four stages of sexual abuse. The use of this fictitious story with general events can give a clear direction of how abuse can occur so easily. Please use the story to guide you to understand and identify how abuse can occur so easily. If your sexual abuse was rape or prostitution, answer the questions from that perspective. Do not skip questions that pertain to you, as almost all of them fit anyone of these forms of sexual abuse.

Stage I: The Set Up

As a young girl, Jane was lonely. Her parents both worked very hard to provide a home for her and her brothers, but most of the time the children were home alone. Jane, being the youngest, was cared for by her older brothers, but they were boys and not interested in the same things she was. She spent many of her days alone in her room playing with games or on her cell phone talking to her friends. The physical contact with people was rarely a part of her life once she was home from school.

The weekends were much the same. Friday nights did not consist of much family interaction -- her parents rarely came home from their jobs before 8:00 pm. Saturday mornings was a time to sleep in and "recoup" from a hard work week. Some Saturdays, Jane's mother would take her shopping or to a movie, but most of the time it was her parents "date day" so they could keep their marriage fresh and their love intact. Jane's brothers played sports on the weekends with their friends, but because Jane was only 12 years old, she was not allowed to go with them for fear that someone would kidnap her when the boys were not looking. Sundays were Church and then back home to prepare for the week ahead. Jane was lonely and desperately wanted attention from her parents, especially her dad, but they were all too busy to hear her silent cries to be noticed.

One day, her neighbor, Mr. Smith, was in the back yard working. Seeing that Jane was alone and looking lonely, he invited her to come into his yard with him and help him put some of his gardening tools back into his yard shed. Asking permission to go next door or even notify her brothers where she was going did not seem necessary. After all, they were busy watching TV, and she had known this neighbor her entire life. Jane and Mr. Smith carefully returned every tool to its proper place, cleaned and oiled, in a very short amount of time. During this brief work period, Mr. Smith began to question Jane about her family and why she thought her parents worked so late every day. He also asked her questions about how good she must feel about becoming such a beautiful young woman. The attention she was receiving from Mr. Smith made her feel good inside. He noticed her and was complimenting her, which was something that rarely occurred in her own home.

The next day, Jane went into her back yard hoping to see Mr. Smith again. Perhaps she could help him do more work in his yard. As soon as she stepped off her porch, there he was planting flowers in his garden. Once again, Mr. Smith invited her over, and once again, he complimented her on how beautiful she looked. But this time he asked her if she had a boyfriend and had she ever been kissed by him. Answering no, the old man replied, "Too bad, the boys don't know what they are missing." Once again, they returned the tools to the yard shed with great care, but this time as he was cleaning his tools he asked Jane if she would like him to show her how to oil them. Standing close to him and feeling very important, she did everything he told her to do. But Jane never saw Mr. Smith reach around behind her as he pushed his hand into the back of her pants, not too far down, but just enough to rest just above her buttocks. Frozen in fear, Jane never said a word, but continued to work as though nothing was happening to her.

Jane went home that day, sick at her stomach at what had happened in the yard shed, but uncertain if she should tell her brothers. The good feelings that she had for Mr. Smith outweighed her bad feelings; she decided that he really did not mean anything by what he had done. She did like being special enough to him that he allowed her to do something with her time other than sit in her room or watch TV all day. If she told anyone, then she was sure she would never be allowed to go to his house again. The incident would remain a secret. In the act of being set up, Mr. Smith took advantage of Jane in testing her to see how far he could go. He did the obvious.

1.) In relation to your past, is there any part that relates to you? If so, how?

2.) Check off each sentence that applied to you and your experiences. If you have memories other than the ones listed, it is okay.

_____ My life appears normal and good to the people that know me.

_____ My childhood was normal in comparison to most of the people that I know.

_____ The relationship that I have with my family is friendly but distant. We see each other at holidays but rarely talk in between.

_____ My family rarely hugged, kissed, or played together growing up.

_____ I was appreciated only when I accomplished what was expected of me.

_____ My parents/guardians were strict, religious, controlling, conservative, and/or unloving.

_____ My parents/guardians were party people who enjoyed drinking and spending weekends with their friends.

_____ As a family, we were expected to keep family problems to ourselves and never tell an outsider.

_____ I was very lonely the majority of my life.

_____ My parents/guardians used their love as a means of getting me to do what they wanted. If I obeyed, then I was praised and loved. If I disobeyed, then I was shunned and ridiculed.

_____ I did my best to keep everyone happy in my home.

_____ I did not care what anyone did as long as I was not the focus of attention.

_____ The weight of being an adult weighed heavily upon me, causing me to eventually give up being a child.

_____ Whenever my family was home, I would avoid them to keep from drawing attention to myself.

_____ I feel as though there are two of me, one on the inside that no one knows and one on the outside that everyone knows.

3.) Complete the sentences below that apply to you.

Within my family, I played the part of an adult by…

The physical boundaries that should have been honored were …

My mental boundaries, thoughts and feelings, were changed by …

Over time, I became unable to know what was good or bad for me in relation to …

Over time, I became numb to my feelings by …

4.) When you think of all the emotions that you are feeling right now, how do you feel? Write out anything that comes into your mind.

Stage II: The Test

In the story of Jane and Mr. Smith, Jane made the decision to remain quiet about the intimate encounter between herself and Mr. Smith. Jane knew it was wrong for this man to put his hand down her pants and touch her -- she had been taught by her parents to tell if anyone touched her in this way, but to tell meant to not have any kind of relationship with him. She wanted attention more than she wanted to tell. Besides, he would probably never do it again and it was only on the small of her back. "He didn't really touch my privates", was the excuse she used over and over again to herself so she did not have to tell anyone.

On the other hand, Mr. Smith was waiting to see what would happen. Would someone come to his home and accuse him of touching this child? Would she tell on him? Would she keep the incident to herself? If any one of these questions were answered for Mr. Smith, through her silence he would know that Jane was a secret keeper. This made an open door for him to spend more time with her with no fear of being told on by Jane.

5.) Do you remember your abuser touching you in the beginning in a way that would be considered bad, but not criminal, to some? If so, what did the person do to you?

Jane was receiving the attention from Mr. Smith that she craved. The attention she was receiving was a reward and an offer of relationship with an older man whom she looked up to.

6.) Did you receive special privileges, gifts, rewards of time, special relationships, or safety, in exchange for your silence or keeping the secret? If so, how did you feel about it then? How do you feel about it now?

7.) What mental and physical reactions are you having right now as you recall these feelings?

Over time, the closeness that Mr. Smith developed with Jane grew and trust was established. The incident in the yard shed had not been repeated, and she had let her guard down when she was with him. Now her parents were aware of the time she was spending with Mr. Smith -- they even let him know how much they appreciated the grandfather figure he had become to their daughter. Given permission to spend all of the time she wanted with him, Jane could not wait for the weekends when he would take her to the garden store to buy more plants. Afterwards they would always stop at the store and get ice cream and a coke, even though her parents did not approve of her drinking sodawater. It was their secret and he would not tell on her for drinking one was his weekly promise.

8.) Do you remember your abuser using your secrets to make you dependent on him/her as the secret keeper?

9.) How did you feel, knowing that you were sneaking around and that someone was willing to keep your secret? If this did not happen to you, then how do you feel when someone keeps your secrets?

10.) How do you feel now about the secrets that were shared between you and the abuser or between you and someone else? (For Jane, it was her secret of disobeying her parents' wishes and his secret of touching her.)

The weeks passed for Jane very quickly, but then a new thing happened. One day, Mr. Smith took her to the garden store, but on their way to get their ice cream he had reached across the seat and put his hand on her leg. Next, he reached up and ran his hand under her shirt telling her once again that she was growing up to be a very beautiful young woman. The touch of his hand was gentle, and a strange feeling ran through her, but once again, she was frozen in fear and unsure of what to do. As fast as he started, he stopped leaving her stunned and unsure of herself. The rest of the trip went exactly the way

                    Caught in the Acts of Grace Women's Bible

it always did. They bought ice cream and a coke, and he teased her for not obeying her parents' wishes as she drank the cup dry.

That night she lay in her bed, thinking about his actions and his knowledge of her secret. Her parents had been very angry with her brother once for bringing home a leftover bottle of soda water from a party. They told him that he should know better and poured the entire bottle down the drain. Fear of receiving the same reaction made her unsure of her next move. Should she tell now or remain silent? Would her parents be mad at her, or would they make her confront Mr. Smith? Would they take his word over hers or blame her for making friends with him to start with?

11.) Do you remember being touched by your abuser in an inappropriate way; and how did you feel when it happened?

12.) How do you feel about yourself when you think about the trust that you placed in the person who abused you?

13.) If you felt feelings of pleasure when you were being touched, do you feel shame and guilt for those feelings?

14.) Do you know that God created you for touch and pleasurable feelings associated with touch? If you are feeling guilty for those feelings, how can you change your opinion of the shame associated with touch?

Stage III: The Act

All the next week and the week after, Jane tried to not think of Mr. Smith's actions in the truck that day. The following week, this man she looked up to was back to his normal ways of teaching Jane how to garden. Once again, they went on their weekend outing, but this time they did not need anything at the garden store. Mr. Smith told her that they would just go for the ice cream and coke today.

As they drove, Jane noticed that the regular route that they took to the ice cream parlor looked different from how she remembered it before. But, being only 12, she shrugged it off thinking it seemed different only because they were going straight from home and not from the store. Soon they arrived at an isolated, abandoned house in the middle of a thicket of woods. Mr. Smith asked her to get out of the truck. He had some flowers in the back of the house that he had planted as a child her age, and he wanted to show them to her. As they rounded the back of the house, Mr. Smith took Jane by the arm and gently guided her into the house………….. !

An hour later, they arrived at the ice cream parlor and once again, he teased her about hiding her secret about drinking Coke. This time, there was a change in the way that Mr. Smith looked at Jane, and she was very frightened. The entire lower part of her body ached and hurt in a way that made her want to cry, but she did not dare for fear that someone would ask her why she was crying.

15.) Do you remember how you felt during the abuse? Describe it the best you can; in your body, your emotions, you were present but in your mind, out of body.

16.) What did you usually do after the incident was over?

17.) Did you feel, all at the same time toward your abuser, both disgust and wanting, hatred and friendship? Did you fear losing their love or friendship?

18.) Did you have feelings of betrayal or self-blame because your body may have responded with pleasure during the abuse?

19.) With touch there is usually a sensation of pleasure. If you do not have a memory of a pleasurable feeling, which of the following did you feel?

    _____ Frozen fear

    _____ Physical pain

    _____ Ignoring any feeling; split of the mind from the body in order to be numb

    _____ Extreme anger

    _____ Other, explain……

20.) After going back into your memories of your abuse, how are you feeling right now?

Stage IV: Manipulation and Management

Leaving the ice cream parlor, Mr. Smith drove home, once again on a route that was unfamiliar to Jane. The fear and uncertainty that she had felt in the past spilled over into shock and numbness at the things done to her, and that he made her do, left a sick feeling inside of her.

As they drove, Mr. Smith began talking to her in a low, soothing tone, coaxing her to talk to him for the first time since they left the old house. He reminded Jane of how much fun they had planting the garden and how much she had learned. He played on the thoughts of the beauty they had created together picking out different flowers and how she had chosen most of the colors they enjoyed now. He explained that he had kept her secret from her parents all of this time; now he expected her to keep his. The reminder of how angry her parents would be at her due to weekly disobedience of the family rules would be equally as bad as the anger they would feel toward her if she told on him. He would make sure they understood she was the one who started all of the deception.

Turning into the drive of Mr. Smith's home, Jane slowly slid out of the passenger seat and shut the door, not looking at Mr. Smith. As she turned to walk into her home she heard him say, "See you next weekend, Jane!"

Inside her home, as she passed through the kitchen, Jane's mother looked at her daughter's face and came to her immediately. Placing her hand on Jane's forehead to check for a fever, she asked Jane if she was feeling okay. Jane feebly replied that she had a stomach ache and felt like throwing up. Both of those things were true -- she did throw up at the old house when she was allowed outside. Promising her daughter some homemade chicken soup, Jane's mother helped her daughter into bed and kept the boys quiet so Jane could rest and recover from her illness the remainder of the weekend.

21.) Was there a time when you felt the need to hide the abuse, in turn covering up who your abuser was and what he/she was doing to you? What did you do or say to accomplish these things?

22.) Were there threats or promises associated with the abuse? Did you tell someone anyway? Were you believed and, if not, what did you do?

23.) Now that the abuse is in the past, how do you feel about hiding the abuse?

24.) In covering the abuse, or coping with the abuse if you told and no one believed you, what have you done in an effort to make a good life for yourself?

25.) Has your past abuse made you a different person than you might have been had you never been abused? In what ways do you believe you are different?

26.) In the overall picture of your life, do you believe God has taken care of you?

    Yes   No

27.) As you moved through the questions in this chapter, are there any circumstances that have become clearer to you about yourself, your family and your abuse situation?

    Yes   No

28.) In the stages of the abuse: The Set Up, The Test, The Act, Manipulation and Management, in what order would you put your own abuse? Perhaps you were taken straight from the act to manipulation and management, or the set up lasted for a long time and stopped after the test.

29.) Is there anything more you can think of at this time that would be helpful to you and your personal discovery of how an abuser was able to abuse you and keep you in silent chains all of these years? Use the space below to write your thoughts.

Tamar, Daughter of King David

The story that we have just read occurred in modern times. The Bible offers many real life situations similar to those in today's world; therefore, we can find a duplicate story to Jane's. The Old Testament contains a similar story of a young girl who was also abused. As you read through the account of her life, consider the stages of abuse that you have learned. Tamar was a young Princess and daughter of King David.

Read 2 Samuel 13:1-22 in your Bible. Next reread these verses using this verse by verse commentary.

Verse 1 - Absalom, Tamar, and Amnon are brothers and sister. Absalom and Tamar are full siblings, and Amnon is a half-brother by a different mother.

Verse 2 - Amnon became very obsessed with Tamar in a lustful way and became distressed. But because she was a Princess, and was protected as royalty from all men, he could not touch her, or he would, by law, be killed even though he was the heir to his father's throne.

Verse 3-5 - Amnon and his cousin, Jonadab, who was crafty, devised a plan to get Tamar away from the palace and the protection of her father, and did it in a way that involved King David himself.

Verse 6 - When King David came to see his oldest son, he realized that there was something wrong with him. He had genuinely lost weight; therefore, he was losing his strength. Being a good dad to his kids, he listened to Amnon when he requested that Tamar be sent to his house to cook a meal for him. His health was a priority to the King.

Verse 7 - King David told his young daughter, Tamar, to go to her brother's home and feed him.

Verse 8-9 - As Tamar was cooking food for Amnon, he was laying down apparently in the kitchen watching her. But after the meal was ready and set before him, he refused to eat and ordered everyone to leave the room.

Verse 10 - As was previously planned with his cousin, Amnon told her to take the food into his bedroom, so she could feed him in there. Being obedient to the future king, she did exactly what she was told.

Verse 11 - When they were in the bedroom, Amnon grabbed her and began to force her to have sex with him.

Verse 12-13 - She tried to stop him by reminding him that to touch her was a disgraceful thing, meaning he could be killed for breaking the law. But he didn't stop. So she tried another tactic, marriage. In those times, it was normal for brothers and sisters to marry. If he had gone to his father to start with and asked for Tamar's hand in marriage, King David would have given her to him. But he did not love her. He lusted after her; therefore, marriage was never a part of the plan.

Verse 14 - He raped her.

Verse 15-16 - After his lust was satisfied, he hated her with the same intensity that he lusted after her. She was no longer a virgin, but he could have kept her as a wife. He rejected her pleas not to send her away. Tamar worried because the act could bring about a terrible curse since it was contrary to the law (Deut. 22:29). Amnon refused to listen to any of Tamar's reasoning.

Verse 17 - Amnon then gave her the final insult. He called his servant to come into the bedroom and remove her from his house. The virgin daughter of King David had now been unwillingly stripped of her virginity and was being treated as a commoner by Amnon's servants. Even the servants in his home believed that she had seduced him in his illness and were no longer treating her with the dignity that she had from them only hours before. Before the rape, no servant would have dared to lay a hand on her, much less throw her out of the front door of the house and lock the door behind her as though she were a prostitute.

Verse 18-19 - Tamar was grief stricken by the shame that was now on her and the curse of no longer being worthy to marry anyone but Amnon since that was whom she had made her blood covenant with when her virginity was lost. She behaved in a normal Jewish grief ritual by putting ashes on her head and tearing her robe. The robe that she tore was one that was unique to only the virgin daughters of the King. She no longer had the right to wear it.

Verse 20 - Absalom found his sister in her grief-stricken hysteria and asked her what happened. Once he confirmed what had happened to her, he reassured her that everything would be taken care of once King David found out that he had not only been tricked by his son, but Amnon had also broken the law. Tamar was taken care of for the rest of her life by her brother Absalom.

Verse 21- King David, dad, found out about what had happened to his daughter and who did it. He knew that he had been the one to send her to Amnon's house, so he carried guilt in this also. He could have made Amnon marry Tamar. He could have obeyed the Law and had Amnon put to death as was commanded. Instead, he just got mad and did nothing to remedy or end the whole situation. Life went on in the palace as though nothing had ever happened, except for Absalom and Tamar.

Verse 22 - From that day on Absalom never spoke good things or bad things about Amnon. His hatred ran so deep that he was quietly waiting for the day that he could avenge his sister. He never forgot his father's refusal to protect his sister.

2 Samuel 13:23-33 - It took Absalom two years of waiting before his day finally arrived, and he killed his brother Amnon for forcing himself on Tamar.

When you were writing out your abuse story, it could have been told a lot like Tamar's abuse story. What is the difference between Tamar and us? We live under Grace to help us to forgive and be forgiving.

Not many people realize that the Bible would have recorded someone's life that involved such treachery, especially in the family of King David who was in the lineage of Jesus Christ. In the Old

Testament we can find not only the pain of a family, but also the triumphs. David was also called by God, "a man after God's own heart." He made numerous mistakes with his family, but he never lost his humility and was always willing to ask God to forgive him from a broken heart, not a deceitful heart.

In your pain of remembering the very thing that you have tried so hard to not think about for all of these years, know that you are not alone. Tamar was never left alone in her sorrow and grief and neither will you be.

As I read and learned about how a person can set up and abuse another, for the first time I began to have feelings rise up inside of me that I did not care for. Rage, fear, disbelief, and curiosity. A "how could you" attitude, "good night I was set up," "why did this happen to me," "where were my protectors." I wondered "why didn't _______________________ stop this when I told them," but most overwhelmingly – my being was drained. Who am I now? That thought seemed to set me back, my mind shut down. Perhaps you feel like I did, perhaps not. In any case, there are reactions brought to the table of our healing in this chapter.

Not only, "Who am I now," came to my mind but other thoughts as well. What do I do with the new information, the reality of manipulation with intent, that now fits my story of abuse? Who cares what others think anymore. What do I think? Now I understand so much more than I ever have, it is beginning to make sense to me! I do not feel any better, but there is a new logic to this mess now! Can this information really allow me to shift any part of the responsibility of the abuse from myself to the abuser? All of these questions have answers, but my heart aches too much right now to focus on any one of them.

At this point, the temptation to quit and walk away is so tempting that the taste of freedom may make your mouth water, like the thought of sucking on a lemon. It may be refreshing but would be, nonetheless, bitter. Why start this journey only to quit and go back to where you were, now angrier because of the knowledge you have now attained?

Dear God,

In Jesus' Name, Amen

REMINDER: Please remember to Journal daily …

Chapter 3

Isn't It A Shame?

Who I Am In Christ

Read daily. Put your name in the blank.

The Word of God Says...

_____________is Created in the image of God by...Psalm 119:73;

_____________is Promised "rest"...Exodus 33:14; Hebrews 4:9

_____________is "Chosen" by Christ...John 15: 16; Ephesians 1:4

_____________is Protected by God... Deuteronomy 7:6-8; Joshua 1:3-9

_____________is Forgiven...Hebrews 9:14; Colossians 1:14; 1 John 2:12

_____________is Blessed...Psalm 1:1-3; Ephesians 1:3

_____________is Able to sleep without fear...Psalm 3:5, 4:8

_____________is the "Apple" of God's eye...Psalm 17:8

_____________is Strong in the Lord...Psalm 18:1-2; Ephesians 6:10

_____________is a Child of God...John 1:12-13; Romans 8:14-15

Objective:

- Understand what causes feelings of devaluation.
- Explore how rejection from one person can affect our other relationships.
- Realize that fear of revelation is a defense mechanism.
- Analyze how one woman in the Bible did not let the fear of exposure keep her from worshiping Jesus.

Inspiration:

> John 4:16-19 (NKJV) Jesus said to her, *"Go, call your husband, and come here."* (17) *The woman answered and said, "I have no husband." Jesus said to her, "You have well said, 'I have no husband,' (18) for you have had five husbands, and the one whom you now have is not your husband; in that you spoke truly." (19) The woman said to Him, "Sir, I perceive that You are a prophet."*

The Journey Continues ...

As what type of person do we portray ourselves? Do we really allow people to see us the way that we are, or do we only present the person that we believe people will want to see and hear? There is a need by most of us to search out what we believe to be socially acceptable, then to adapt that outward appearance to hide the inward person in our heart.

Such was the case with Cyrano de Bergerac, a French soldier and poet who lived in the mid 1600's. Although he was a real person, the fictitious play based upon his life (written and produced by Edmond Rostand) turned him into someone more famous than he really was. The play centers upon Cyrano's love for the fair Roxane. Though Cyrano loves Roxane passionately, embarrassment over his excessively large nose keeps him from expressing his true feelings for Roxane. Instead, Cyrano turns to another man, Christian de Neuvillette, to help him physically woo Roxane. Why? Because, though less articulate than Cyrano, Christian was more conventionally handsome. Eventually, because of the beautiful words Cyrano pens for Christian to speak on his behalf, Roxane falls in love with Christian de Neuvillette, thinking he is Cyrano. You can imagine her disappointment when Roxane discovers the truth - that she has been tricked and lied to.

In the play, Christian is valued for his words and his appearance, whereas Cyrano is devalued because of his large nose. Ironically, the truth is that the actual historical figure that Rostand's character was based upon-Hector-Savinien de Cyrano de Bergerac- did have an overly large nose, but he was also very proud of it. It is only through the hands of the man who wrote the play "Cyrano de Bergerac" that the historical and the fictional Cyrano take completely different roads.

In today's world, we also find hypocritical "Cyrano's." People are tagged as hypocrites when they present themselves as good around certain people, but bad when those people they are trying to impress are no longer around. Like a chameleon, hypocrites change with the crowd. Originally, the word hypocrite meant an actor or someone who pretends to be someone they are not. Over time, the definition of hypocrite became the word. A hypocrite soon came to mean someone we did not want to be while an actor came to mean someone we admire. (If we still used the original meaning of the word we would say our favorite "hypocrite" instead of our favorite "actor").

When we experience a shameful situation in our lives, we sometimes begin to live hypocritically out of fear that we will be devalued by others. We try to avoid or completely shut out of our minds any memory of the traumatic event. Just like cockroaches, we adapt to whatever is happening in order to survive. We become superficial, pretend, act overly-friendly; or we go to the other extreme - we act coldly toward others and avoid them, choose deception and dishonesty, speak with hurtful frankness, and refuse to keep quiet about who we are. Where is the balance between presenting ourselves as hypocrites to avoid devaluation from others and being so honest about ourselves that our own words make us a target for open rebuke?

Do you present yourself to certain people in a manner that could be perceived as being different than you really are on the inside? If you answer "no" or "never", then you have just proven yourself to have a bigger problem than you realize. You are a hypocrite. Everyone would like to say that they are never affected by others and they are in control of their emotions at all times. But the reality is that we all want to be valued and to avoid shame. We fear rejection, we are moved by guilt, and we hide behind the false character we have created for ourselves to play in public. This leaves us with a deep suspicion of everyone. We think, "If I am a liar about who I really am on the inside, perhaps others are, too! So whom can I trust when I know no one should trust me?"

A sexually abused person will often behave externally as though nothing is wrong, when all the while internally they are in pain and want to scream for help. This can become such a natural way of life that it turns into a reality for us. Pretense seems normal. Avoidance is our pain reliever. But constantly living on the edge of emotional control and lack of control is tiring. Hyper-vigilance, or waiting for the next thing to happen, keeps our adrenaline at an unhealthy level that robs us of our peace and joy in life.

We also experience embarrassing situations in life that can place at us at a crossroads. Often, the choices we make during these times are based on our emotions at the moment- sometimes we run away or pretend nothing happened. At other times, we face our situation or admit our guilt.

During any given time from my life, I can recall memories of embarrassing things that I have done. I have proudly introduced my brand new brother-in-law by the name of the ex-brother-in-law. I have "accidentally" broken out the back window of a pickup of a friend of the family, then not told anyone it was me that threw the Coke bottle threw the window. The "bottle" should tell you the incident took place a long time ago, but the feeling of embarrassment is still with me. Several times, I have not made it to the bathroom on time, even though I was old enough to know better. I think that I have shared enough that anyone could understand where I am going with this.

• Quickly write about a time when you did something that caused you embarrassment.

                    Caught in the Act of Grace Women's Bible Study

Embarrassment is an issue we all have to face, but dealing with shame is another. Shame causes changes in behavior in order to protect, rather than to serve as a simple cover-up. Shame can be a temporary emotion caused by embarrassment, or it can evolve into something much more complex.

Shame can be defined as involving four elements:

> A. Shame causes avoidance of <u>Exposure</u> – Someone I care about might see.

> B. Shame brings on a <u>Dread of Consequences</u> – Rejection.

> C. <u>Value</u> - an empowering of another to determine our desirability or worth.

> D. Shame avoids <u>Revelation</u> – Don't let those important to me know me!

In order to understand these four elements, we must look at each one briefly. As we do, ask yourself these questions: "Is God the source of my value or am I?" and "If I am forgiven, why do I need to shamefully hide from who I am?"

A. Shame causes avoidance of exposure - Someone I care about might see.

In the Garden of Eden there were two people, Adam and Eve. These two people were the only people in recorded history who actually walked daily and visited with God Himself, face to face.

One day, Eve got into a conversation with Satan, who was disguised as a snake, and was convinced to eat from the very tree that God told her not to eat from (Genesis 3:3). What was the end result? She also fed the fruit to her hubby, Adam, and they both discovered something that they never knew before- they were naked. Everything around them looked different, felt different, and they were now confused and afraid. So what did they do? Compare the shame elements listed above to their situation.

1.) **Read Genesis 3:7-12**.

What was the first thing they experienced? ______________________________

What was the second thing they realized? ______________________________

What did they do next? ______________________________

What did they do when they heard God walking in the garden? ______________________________

Why did they hide? ______________________________

Why was Adam afraid of his friend seeing him? ______________________________

What was the first thing Adam did when God asked him who told him that he was naked?

____

2.) Of all of these questions, which one of the shame experiences was involved?

3.) Have you ever been so embarrassed or ashamed of something you have done, that you immediately blamed someone else? Explain.

God sees our past and all of the stuff built up inside our heart, but He loves us anyway. He values us so much that He is willing to get as intimate with us as we will allow Him. But just like Adam and Eve, when we fear exposure of our flaws, we hide when we believe that He is looking.

Read Ephesians 5:26-27.

4.) What does God want to do for us in verse 26?

5.) What does He want to use to wash us with?

6.) In verse 27, what does He want to do with us after He bathes us?

7.) At the very last part of verse 27, what does He say we are after we are sanctified and washed with His word and presented to Him?

The idea of being given a bath, and then presented to someone, even though it is figurative, can be very intimidating. One of the most vulnerable times in our lives is when we are naked and exposed in the shower. If someone uninvited walks in, we grab for a towel to cover ourselves and begin screaming, "GET OUT!" Because of another time in our lives when we felt the same type of vulnerable exposure -- when we were being abused- situations where we fear exposure or someone finding out will cause us to react and "grab for the towel" or scream "GET OUT".

8.) Do you take a physical bath every day, once a week, once a month, bi-annually, or yearly?

9.) If you are washed with the water of the Word, you can compare this to taking an actual bath. How often are you washed with the Word through devotionals, going to church, going to Bible studies?

10.) Do you smell good or do you stink spiritually?

11.) If someone were to sit close to your spiritual self, what would their opinion be of your spiritual hygiene? "I don't care" doesn't cut it here. Honesty is the only way to get out of your pit and the opinions of others do matter a great deal to us all.

God wants something more. He wants you to not be ashamed and to know that you have great value to Him. He created you and formed you to perfectly match the world in which He placed you. To know how much He loves you requires that you be willing to expose yourself, let others see your flaws, expect to be accepted and not rejected, and then be able to find your value in who God says you are, not in what others say you are.

12.) Read Ezekiel 36:25-27. What do these verses mean to you?

13.) How are you to let go of shame? Read verses 25 and 26 where it says that God will wash you and change you. Did you know you must ask? Now look up and write out Psalm 51:7 and 10.

B. Shame brings on a Dread of Consequences – Rejection.

In the Garden of Eden, Adam blamed the woman first and then God. Eve blamed the snake. In truth, they each decided individually to eat the fruit from the tree and disobey God, but they lied because the fear of being found out and then rejected caused them to lie. In life, people who hate lying will sometimes burst out in the biggest lie they have ever told- then they wonder where in the world the lie came from. Rejection is directly related to shame and shame can be used as an excuse to reject or lie.

For example, I was in a conversation with a member of my husband's family about some personal situations. In the past, I had always felt comfortable talking to her because she was not so churchy that she was unwilling to have a little "edgy" fun- nothing ungodly, just fun. After almost 20 years of relationship with this woman, I was in need of some older Christian woman counsel and figured that she would be a good person to talk to. After spending the evening talking and laughing and waiting until everyone else had gone to bed, I decided to ask for her advice.

I began by telling her the situation with the intent of asking her what I should do. The only problem was that after I shared the situation, she became extremely angry with me and began to accuse me of doing something that I had never dreamed of doing. As the attack continued, my mind froze in fear- I could not believe that this woman whom I had considered to be my friend all of this time was now behaving in a manner that I had never witnessed before and it was all directed at me.

My response to the attack came out of a natural instinct to get out of the line of fire. Fight or flight battled inside of me and my wings sprouted. All I could think of was, "Get me away from her and I will never talk to her about anything personal again. Please God, get her away!" In my state of frozen disbelief, I did exactly what she accused me of - I lied. Oh my word! I lied to get her to stop attacking me. I told her that she was right. I was lying and everything that I said was made up. I was mistaken in all of what I had just said. The only problem was I was not mistaken.

My dilemma then became what to do with the relationship with this family member. The best thing about family is that they make great examples when you are driving a point home and she topped the charts for me. As soon as I could get out of the room with her, I began to think, "What in the world just happened?" I lied about lying? Who does that? The answer is easy- confusion comes when someone feels exposed, fears rejection, then tops it off with allowing the other person to determine their value or worth in the relationship. At that particular moment, I began fearing rejection- not from her, because by then she just looked like a mad old woman, but from my husband. I knew she was one of his favorite family members and by crossing her, I might possibly cross him. Though it did not occur to me at the time, I had not done anything wrong. I had simply been thrust into the position of a victim. Ouch!

The relative's final reaction to my confidence brought about my lying- I was devalued by her. She had chosen not to recognize that I was seeking her advice about my own feelings and that I needed her help to work through those feelings to a good end. She had chosen instead to place more value on her own feelings and become cruel. Unfortunately, that reaction comes from people more often than not. Do not assume that just because a person is an old Christian, they are a wise Christian.

The shame that I encountered through that conversation made me dread knowing that I would have to tell my husband the next morning what had happened the night before. When I did, bless him, he apologized for her behavior, and my value came back!

                    Caught in the Act of Grace Women's Bible Study

14.) Have you ever been in a situation that you reacted in a manner that is not a part of your character at all?

Write down the situation and all of the shame elements that you felt.

15.) Looking back on that situation, is there anything that you could have done differently on your part to change what happened? Be realistic and don't put all of the blame on yourself.

16.) As we look back on some experiences, through the eyes of logic or reality in place of shame-filled memories, some experiences seem smaller than they did to begin with. Is there anything about your situation that does not seem as large now as it once did?

I realize now that I could have changed some things with this member of my husband's family. First, I should not have assumed that the relative loved me as much as they loved someone else or themselves; I should not have expected to be treated with the same amount of respect that she had for my husband just because she was nice to me in the past. My mistake was talking to her about personal problems to start with; especially because those personal problems involved people that she felt more loyal to than me.

C. _Value_ - *an empowering of another to determine our desirability or worth.*

Being a country music fan, I love to listen to really good country music. Many years ago there seemed to be a period of time where the songs became a little too folksy or perhaps whiney for my taste. The male singers that were recording these songs also seemed less than appealing to me. Then one of these less than desirable male singers married a female country singer who was extremely popular and beautiful. Conversations with my friends revolved around, "Why did she marry HIM? Is there something about him that we don't see? Perhaps we should look at him again!" The fact that this man was desired by this woman who was "acceptable" to us made him also acceptable. Now the love story between Tim McGraw and Faith Hill is celebrated. But it took someone claiming him as valuable before we saw his value.

Read Luke 7:36–50.
In this series of scripture verses, the writer tells us about a moment in Jesus' life when a woman who was considered an especially wicked sinner responded to him even though she feared possible

unpleasant consequences. In verse 38, the woman who anointed Jesus' feet with oil and washed them with her tears and hair was a prostitute and was well known in her hometown for her undesirable lifestyle. Her worth at the time in the eyes of many was not much. But to those of us today, her sense of worth is more than valuable - it gives us hope.

This poor woman was the kind of person the "religious" gave up on because it was too hard to help her; instead, she was avoided. Yet she still chose to present herself to Jesus Christ in the house of a Temple priest. The assumption is that the oil she used to anoint Jesus' feet was a year's worth of wages she had earned by sleeping with men. The woman also used her hair as a cloth to help clean Jesus' feet. Odd as this may seem, she had much more than embarrassment at stake in her decision to crash a party where she was neither wanted nor invited.

> • In antiquity, or ancient times, a woman could be divorced by her husband for exposing her hair and face in public. This was a very serious offense.

> • In public, she was touching and kissing a man in to whom she was not married.

> • This woman was willing to expose her sins and herself before the Lord in the presence of men who hated her and could stone her at any time because she was a prostitute.

> • She was willing to show her remorse and repentance no matter who was watching - including the religious people in her town.

What the woman actually did was make the decision that no matter what, she was going to see Jesus. Even if it cost her life, she would give to Him the most precious thing she owned, in the most humble of servant tasks she could think of, by washing His feet with her own hair.

17.) When was the last time you were willing to do something that you knew would cause you ridicule and judgment from others, thereby potentially making you feel devalued? If the answer was never, would you ever be willing to do something that would cause you ridicule and judgment from others?

Caught in the Act of Grace Women's Bible Study

CeCe Winans recorded a song called "Alabaster Box" that was based on Luke 7:36-50; it has incredible meaning to those of us who have accepted Jesus as our Redeemer.

(Ce Ce Winans. "Alabaster Box." Sparrow Records, 10/191999, Wallspring Gospel.)

The room grew still As she made her way to Jesus
She stumbles through the tears that made her blind
She felt such pain, some spoke in anger
Heard folks whisper there's no place here for her kind
Still on she came through the shame that flushed her face
Until at last she knelt before His feet
And though she spoke no words
Everything she said was heard
As she poured her love for the Master From her box of Alabaster

Chorus
And I've come to pour My praise on Him like oil
From Mary's Alabaster Box
Don't be angry if I wash His feet with my tears And I dry them with my hair
You weren't there the night He found me
You did not feel what I felt When He wrapped His loving arms around me
And you don't know the cost of the oil in my Alabaster box

I can't forget the way life used to be
I was a prisoner to the sin that had me bound
And I spent my days Poured my life without measure
Into a little treasure box I thought I'd found
Until the day when Jesus came to me
And healed my soul with the wonder of His touch
So now I'm giving back to Him All the praise He's worthy of
I've been forgiven and that's why I love Him so much.

18.) What was the cost of the oil in your alabaster box and are you willing to pour that pain out onto Jesus' feet to release yourself from the prison of that pain?

19.) Explain what you understand about the song and the woman's need to overcome her sense of shame in order to express her love for her Master, no matter who was looking.

Devaluation and Sexual Malfunctioning

NOTE - If you are a single, please skip down to question "a)" below. This section is for marital relationships only. In no way is sex outside of the marital relationship encouraged nor should it be discussed in an intimate way. In fact, God calls premarital sex or extramarital sex, sin; therefore we call it sin. But these are issues that must be addressed within the vow of marriage as a healthy and needed expression of intimacy in the relationship.

Feeling devaluated in relationships is a terrible way to live. To not address this at this point in the Bible study would leave a sense of incompleteness in the study. The overall expression of devaluation in a relationship with a man and woman is impenetrable for many women. The idea that some women have concerning the enjoyment of sex because of their past is not always physical, but emotional.

If there is a physical or hormonal issue with sex, such as pain or dryness during intercourse, then please go see your doctor. These are issues that should have medical attention.

If the issue with no fulfillment or dissatisfaction with sex is based on a feeling of not being loved, being used as an object to fulfill a need, the emotional connection between a man and wife is not being met prior to sex, respect has never been established or maintained, or just feeling like you are dirty for allowing a man to use you in this way, this is where we will briefly address this issue. Please understand that there are no magic cures for marital strife or sexual dysfunction. Both require a sincere inward evaluation of self and desire to change, no matter what the other partner is choosing to do. Because of the intimacy of marriage, if trust has not been established in a relationship, this may be a challenge that is much more difficult to obtain. But with both spouses working hard toward change, a new and fulfilling relationship is possible.

a.) **Read Matthew 23:11-12**. Please write out these two verses. Realize that the definition of a servant is a person who serves, not a slave. A slave can be a servant, but a servant is not a slave unless he or she is a bond slave.

b.) **Read Ephesians 5: 25-33**. How many times is a man commanded to love his wife? Who is the example of who he is commanded to love his wife like? What did Christ do to express His love for His bride (the church)?

Many women say that these verses are conveniently quoted by men who want to control them by reminding them that they are to submit to their husbands as a service to the Lord, because he is the head of the wife just like Christ is the head of the church. The fact that Christ loved the church so much that He took an enormous amount of abuse from it and eventually died for it is often overlooked.

c.) **Read Ephesians 5:22-24, 33**. What is a woman commanded to do for her husband? How many times is she told to do this?

d.) **Read 1 Peter 3:1-7**. Women are told to be submissive to their husbands in these verses, but in verse 7, what does God call the man and women together? If the man does not treat his wife with this kind of respect, what does God do to him?

e.) **Read Genesis 1: 26-27.** Did God give dominion to the man only or did He say "them"? Therefore, do men and women have equal dominion and rule over the earth?

f.) **Read Ephesians 5:21.** "Be subject to one another out of reverence for Christ (the Messiah, the Anointed One)." Who are we to be subject to? Why are we to be subject to one another?

g.) Write the definition of submission.

Many times in marital relationships, one spouse will dominate the other. The continual reminder of control and servitude is portrayed in daily life. Comments such as "woman's work," "what have you been doing all day," "you never listen to me," "I don't care what you think," all wound deeply.

h.) Because there is confusion between submission and servitude, write the definition of servitude.

i.) Are submission, servitude or subjection the same thing?

Trust, intimacy, willingness to give in the act of sexual intimacy, emotional connection that is necessary for both the male and female, feeling valued and treasured, putting the others needs above your own - all of these are needed before sex will ever be satisfactory. Sex is nothing more than the act of procreation in the physical form. In the spiritual, it is the command by God for the two becoming one in the flesh. In the mental, it is the point of a man leaving ALL other people in his life to make his wife the most important PERSON to him, but not his god. To the woman, it is where she leaves behind who she once was to become what her husband needs. The Amplified Bible calls it adapting herself to her husband in I Peter 3. In the emotional, a woman must be satisfied first before she can give herself over to a man in the physical; it is at that time that he is emotionally filled.

Who fills the woman emotionally? The man. How can he fill her emotionally? By letting her know that he loves and cherishes her like Christ loves the Church. This looks different for everyone. Some need touch, some attention through talking, some need gifts, some want help around the house doing odd jobs or cleaning chores, some need cards in the mail, some need weekend get-a-ways, some need time to themselves, some need weekly dates; all need their spouses close by. All need to know that they are more important than friends, extended family, hobbies or work. We should all care enough about the person that we have vowed to be our closest friend and mate to find out what way they need to feel love - then do it with no strings attached.

The confusion that occurs between husbands and wives is that each does not know what the other wants. Have you ever been given a gift and wondered why it was given to you when it was nothing that you would remotely want? But the person who gave the gift really wanted it, so they decided that you did, too. Then, when you didn't react as excitedly as they were about it, feelings got hurt and words were said that caused damage all because we try to give to others what we would like to have. What about purchasing a gift that is suitable to others tastes, but not your own?

I hate the sight and smell of raw oysters; it makes my gag reflex begin to pulse. But every time I go out to eat with my husband at a seafood restaurant, he orders a dozen on the half shell. While we wait for our food, I cover my eyes, push away from the table as far as I can and cringe as he happily eats his oysters. How nasty can you get!!! But why do I sit through this culinary delight of his? Why does he order them all of the time when he knows that they really disgust me? Because we both know that it is not about us -- it is about the other. If he wants them, get them. But don't expect me to eat them and please don't expect me not to make faces about it the whole time they are on the table. Raw oysters are suitable to his taste - it is a gift that I give him by tolerating them.

Go to marriage classes, get counseling, quit being self- centered with your needs, do whatever it takes to change what marriage is about. When you learn that God is your value calculator - not your past sexual abuse-then and only then will you learn that it is not the sex that you hate, but the way you feel in your marriage relationship toward the person you are having sex with. Sex is the ultimate giving of self in the most intimate fashion there is. It exposes the most vulnerable parts of your body and your soul. To do that in a healthy manner means to have a healthy view of self and your spouse.

None of us can give away what we do not have. If we see no value in ourselves, then others will not see value in us either. If we see no value in ourselves, then we will not treat others as though they have value. This is true not only in marriage relationships, but in all relationships.

By the way Paul made it quite clear that women were to be silent in church. But what was he really speaking of in I Corinthians 14:33-40? He was teaching the members of a church how to conduct a church service with order so everyone is not speaking at once. Did he just randomly throw out a command that women are to be seen and not heard in churches? No! He was teaching the men and the women that during a church service is not the time for everyone to talk; instead, he suggested that people learn to take turns or wait until returning home to ask questions. He was also teaching that men were to teach the men and women the women, because we are all so different from one another.

The Bible also clearly teaches that women are to submit to their husbands as their head, not to men in general. Far too many times men have tried to tell me that I am to submit to them because I am a woman and they are a man. My response is to remind them that they are not my husband and if there is a problem with me, my husband will be the first to let me know. Then I remind them that they are now standing in my space, so please move on.

The fact is that God values men and women equally!

D. Shame avoids Revelation – Don't let those important to me know me!

Revelation in relationships requires honesty. But when one has such a fear of people knowing who they really are on the inside, honesty is something that is not freely given. Thoughts of shame and guilt keep us in a prison inside of our own minds with no hope of being ourselves. We constantly think "no one can know or they may not like me." Sadly enough, people do judge us for our actions whether we intentionally did something or not. The judgmental way we are treated is the harsh reality that makes us want to hide our sin. To be seen as less or unworthy becomes avoided at all costs in order for the guilt to go away.

For over 15 years I told no one in my family about the abuses that I had been through as a young child. There were people in my family that knew, but it was not something that we discussed, only because they could not do anything to help me. Then one day as a young adult, I snapped and blurted it out to my mom. How wounded she was that not only did it happen repeatedly by people she trusted with my safety, but that it happened over such a long period of time - about seven years. Revelation for her brought a great deal of pain and anger. My father, when told, blamed me for the abuses. Revelation for him caused me pain. From that point on, to tell meant the risk of judgment and rejection from others.

I believed that when I married my husband, a minister, I was now expected to be pure as the driven snow and have no flaws in my character. After all, ministers' wives cannot be victims of sexual abuse, or have an abortion or a sordid past such as mine. Revelation now meant that I would be an embarrassment for my husband, but worse yet, God.

Unfortunately, my past became an issue for some people once we knew it was time to stop hiding behind my silence and we spoke out. But God was not embarrassed by me; He loved me deeply and was very proud of me. It was people who caused me to be afraid and wounded me regularly during that time in my life. Knowing that God would never leave me and that my husband and children were staying close by me was an incredible source of strength.

20.) **Read Matthew 23:24-28**. What did Jesus call those who looked one way on the outside, but were another way on the inside?

21.) Although He was talking to the religious people of the day, do you know people now who are like these He was talking to? Are you like those people?

22.) Have you allowed a fear of people knowing the real you (or uncertainty of how they will treat you after they know certain information about you) to stop you from doing the things you feel God has called you to do?

23.) Here is a test to help you determine your level of fear of people. The more yes's, the more the fear.

When you walk into a room with people you don't know, do you hang back instead of expecting people to want to talk to you and get to know you?

        No   Yes

Do you hold back when certain questions are being asked about your personal life?

        No   Yes

Does your stomach tighten at the thought of standing before people and telling about yourself and your past?

        No   Yes

If you could go on a trip with a group of people and you knew none of them, would you go anticipating the adventure of making new friends? Or would you simply stay home until people you knew were going "so you could have more fun."

        No, stay and wait   Yes, go freely making friends

Read Revelation 12: 11, 17.

24.) The devil is overcome by the word of what?

25.) In verse 17, who was he enraged with?

26.) Also in verse 17, who did he go to make war with - who will keep what and have what?

As Christians, we often believe we can hide what we feel is wrong with us and hope no one will ever find out. But just as God saw Adam and Eve's nakedness in the Garden of Eden before they did, He knows everything already. In light of this, we should know that people will forgive us as readily as God, so we should also forgive ourselves when we mess up.

27.) Have you ever had to keep a secret other than the secret of your sexual abuse? If sexual abuse is a level 10 secret, what level would most of your secrets be?

28.) With God there are no secrets, level one or level ten, He knows them all. **Read Hebrews 4: 11-16**. Write out verse 16.

Right now, stop and ask God to change and renew your heart from a heart of stone to a heart of flesh.

Dear God,

In Jesus' Name, Amen.

REMINDER: Please remember to Journal daily …

Chapter 4

Why Me?

Who I Am In Christ

Read daily. Put your name in the blank.

The Word of God Says...

______________________ is washed clean from my sins...Isaiah 1:18

______________________ is always in God's thoughts...Psalm 139:17-18

______________________ is loved by God...Jeremiah 31:3; Romans 8:37-39

______________________ is the salt of the earth...Matthew 5:13-14

______________________ is valued by God...Matthew 10:29-31

______________________ is at peace with God...Romans 5:1

______________________ is dead to sin...Romans 6:1-18

______________________ is the temple of the Holy Spirit...1 Corinthians. 6:19-20

______________________ is a new creature in Christ...2 Corinthians 5:17

______________________ is crucified with Christ...Galatians 2:20

Objective:

- Begin to realize that even Jesus asked why
- Begin to realize that even Job asked why
- Know where God was
- Why do I hurt when others hurt me

Inspiration:

Isaiah 55:8 (NKJV) *For My thoughts are not your thoughts, nor are your ways My ways" says the Lord.*

The Journey Continues …

Many years ago I had a huge struggle with depression. We had moved into an area where I knew no one, my husband was gone most of the time, all day, and my children were preschoolers. I felt isolated and very lonely. Life had begun to feel as though it was swallowing me up. I wanted so much to make friends, but it was very difficult - our church was 20 miles away and most of the people who attended it were seasonal.

I noticed I was becoming increasingly depressed -- until one day when I had had enough. My husband was home for part of the day, playing with our children in the backyard. Suddenly, a severe spring storm blew in from the north and he began gathering them up to hustle them back into the house. I, on the other hand, declared, "I'm going for a walk!" His voice filled with concern, he explained that the lightning was very severe and I should come inside right away.

I ignored him. With my head and shoulders hanging and tears streaming down my cheeks, I walked into the pasture behind our house. The crisp wind blew my hair. The lightning danced across the pine trees and spider legs streaked the sky. Further and further into the pasture I went, walking toward the storm, not caring if I was struck by lightning.

Finally, I stopped and looked up toward the heavens. Sobbing in loneliness and despair, I yelled to God, "Why am I like this?" and "What is wrong with me?" The wind was blowing very hard, the sky was boiling in black clouds, and the lightning was both mesmerizing and frightening at the same time. Then, just like Elijah when he came out of the cave and waited to hear from God, I heard a still small voice speak to my heart.

The voice from Heaven said, "Darla, I made you the way you are and I like you." My Creator said to me the one thing that would bring me the most comfort. Just because it seemed like bad things chased after me like the hounds of hell, there was nothing wrong with me nor was I unlikable. I was me and God liked me the way I was. In fact, He created me the way I was and still am. Joy filled up inside of me, turning my tears of sorrow into tears of relief. Then the next thing that God said sent me scrambling. He said, "Now get back to the house before you get hit by lightning." He never misses an opportunity for humor in the midst of my distress!

As I walked into the house, with a smile on my face, my husband held me in sweet relief. Sometimes in the storms of life, a good old fashioned thunderstorm can bring things back into perspective.

"Why me?" turned into "I made you the way you are and I like you."

Jesus Asked Why

1.) **Read Mark 9:12**. What does it mean when it says, "How is it written concerning the Son of Man?" Now look up Psalm 22:6 and write it out.

2.) Mark 9:12 talks about Jesus suffering many things and being utterly despised, treated with contempt and rejected. David also felt those same feelings brought on by others in Psalm 22:6. What part of verse 6 is the same as Mark 9:12? Write out the answer.

3.) **Now read all of Psalm 22**. This Psalm is filled with many prophecies concerning the death of the Messiah. Victims of sexual abuse often ask the question, "Why did this happen to me?" Write out Psalm 22:1.

4.) Did Jesus ask "Why are You letting this happen?", or did He ask "Where are You?"

When bad things happen to innocent people or things happen that we wish had not when it started out "not so innocent", we ask God to give an account of Himself. Our pain needs an answer to the question "Why me?" When we don't get a satisfactory answer we may begin to fight God by avoiding church or other Christians, self-abusive behaviors, or by believing we are damaged in some way or unworthy.

The root to this particular way of thinking is not "Why me?" but "Why am I not valuable enough for God to keep this from happening to me? What is wrong with me?" To keep all the past pain in perspective it must not be substituted with the wrong question. No one wants an answer to the real question in the back of their mind, "Is there something so wrong with me that I am not worthy of protection from God?" The pain of that question runs so deeply that we ask the simple and incomplete "Why me?" questions.

Caught in the Act of Grace Women's Bible Study

Job Asked Why

5.) **Read Job 7:17-21**. Remember that Job is deeply in the middle of all of his problems at this point. Much of his speeches are questions that he asks as he vents his frustration. He is not really blaming God for his misery, but he does allow his grief and pain to speak, making his questions seem the same then as they are for many today. Summarize what Job is saying in these verses, paying special attention to verses 20 and 21.

6.) Who does Job believe is the cause of his problems, himself or God? Why do you believe this?

Job 33:12-14. (AMP) *"I reply to you, Behold, in this you are not just; God is superior to man. (13) Why do you contend against Him? For He does not give account of any of His actions. [Sufficient for us it should be to know that it is He Who does them.] (14) For God [does reveal His will; He] speaks not only once, but more than once, even though men do not regard it [including you, Job]."*

In the previous verses it sounds as though God allows pain in our lives, as though He plans them on purpose. But that is not true.

7.) Fill in the blank.   Job 33:13 (AMP), *"For He does not give account for any of ______________."*

8.) **Read Job 1:9-12 and Job 2:1-7**. Who is attacking Job?

Satan is the adversary and accuser of the brethren, or in modern language, the accuser of us. God created us with the ability to make choices so that we can choose to serve Him or not to serve Him. He does not want mindless, emotionless, robotic people who are forced to worship. Everyone feels special when they know they are chosen in a relationship - it is the same with God. He wants to be chosen and worshipped out of love and desire for Him. In order to have a choice for good there must be an opposing force or choice for evil. No choice is a choice when there is only one option. Bad things happen to the good or innocent people of this world because someone had a choice and they chose evil over good. They chose the devil's way over God's way.

Why did God allow Satan to test Job? Because God knew Job's heart and He knew that Job had a weakness that needed to be dealt with - fear. But He also knew that Job loved Him more than life itself. Job had to make a choice - fear of evil or love of God.

9.) **Read Job 3:24-26**. What does Job say that indicates his weakness?

Not only did God know that Job worshipped Him because of an unhealthy fear, but so did Satan. Job's weakness immediately came to the surface when Satan began his attack on Job.

10.) Did God protect Job during this time of trials? How?

11.) **Read John 14:27**. What does it say about fear?

12.) **Read John 14:30-31**. Who is in control in reality?

Where Was God?

13.) Write out Matthew 27:46.

As Jesus was hanging on the cross, there was a moment in time when He became sin for us. He did this by taking every bad thing that we do, our sin, upon Himself. We interpret Matthew 27: 46 to say that God cannot look at sin. Therefore, at the point of death, Jesus' final cry was "Where are you God?" Jesus was alone on the cross so that we would never have to be alone now. No sin, not even someone else's (your abuser's sin), can keep God from being with you.

14.) Do you understand that you were never alone when you were being abused? How does that make you feel?

Caught in the Act of Grace Women's Bible Study

15.) **Read Isaiah 53:3-6** (NKJV). The Bible says that Jesus is a "man of sorrows and acquainted with grief." In the midst of our sorrows and grief, we have an ally who also was "despised and we did not esteem him", but in verses 4-6 it also gives us promises.

Fill in the blanks using the New King James version or as close as you can with your Bible:

Surely He has borne our ___________ and carried our _______________; Yet we ______________ Him _______________, smitten by God, and afflicted. But He was ________________ for our transgressions. He was _________ for our iniquities; the chastisement for our ____________________ was upon Him. And by His _______ we are _____________. All _______ like sheep have gone astray; we have turned, everyone, to his ___________________; And the Lord has laid on Him the iniquity of us all.

16.)   God Himself understands your pain and has already experienced what you have felt or are feeling. Write out your thoughts about your understanding of this.

17.) **Read all of Psalm 23.** Which verse is the most significant to you and why?

Psalm 23:4(NIV) *"Even though I walk through the valley of the shadow of death, I will fear no evil, for You are with me; Your rod and Your staff, they comfort me."*

 In verse 4, does God say to stop and hang out in the valley of your life or does He say to keep walking through? When we walk through a valley, eventually there is another side that we will come to. Valleys are always surrounded by mountains; therefore, there is always an up after a down. We will not stay in a valley if we continue to move forward. God's rod brings discipline while we are walking through our valleys and with His staff He leads us. Most importantly, we have nothing to fear because He never leaves us to walk through our hurts or our healing alone. He is always with us even when we don't think He is.

When Others Hurt Us

18.) Mark 9:12 says "be treated with contempt." **Read Luke 23:6-12.** What did Herod expect from Jesus due to His reputation?

19.) What did Jesus do when He was in Herod's presence?

20.) What was Herod's attitude toward Jesus after the interview?

21.) What did the soldiers do to Jesus?

22.) How do you think Jesus felt toward the soldiers, Herod and Pilate while this was happening? Remember, He is both God and Man.

Read Philippians 2:1-13 (NKJV).

*1) Therefore **if** there is any consolation in Christ, if any comfort of love, if any fellowship of the Spirit, **if** any affection and mercy, 2) fulfill my joy by being like-minded, having the same love, being of one accord, of one mind. 3) **Let** nothing be done through selfish ambition or conceit, but in lowliness of mind let each esteem others better than himself. 4) **Let** each of you look out not only for his own interests, but also for the interests of others. 5) **Let** this mind be in you which was also in Christ Jesus, 6) who, being in the form of God, did not consider it robbery to be equal with God, 7) but made Himself of no reputation, taking the form of a bondservant, and coming in the likeness of men. 8) And being found in appearance as a man, He humbled Himself and became obedient to the point of death, even the death of the cross. 9) **Therefore** God also has highly exalted Him and given Him the name which is above every name, 10) that at the name of Jesus every knee should bow, of those in heaven, and of those on earth, and of those under the earth, 11) and that every tongue should confess that Jesus Christ is Lord, to the glory of God the Father. 12) **Therefore**, my beloved, as you have always obeyed, not as in my presence only, but now much more in my absence, work out your own salvation with fear and trembling; 13) for it is God who works in you both to will and to do for His good pleasure.*

23.) Write out the phrase behind each word "if" in verse 1.

If   If

If   If

The results of the "ifs" are the "Let" in verses 3-5. Write out each "let" phrase.

Let

Let

Let

The conclusions are in verses 9-13 in the "Therefore". Sum them up and write out the conclusion phrase.

Servant or Slave

The Biblical definition of the word "bondservant" is one who gives himself up to the will of another without any idea of bondage. (Paul intimates in Romans 1:1 that he had been formerly a "bond slave" to Satan, but is now bought by Christ and is a willing slave, bound to a new Master.)

Servanthood and caring for others more than oneself can be hard from time to time. The feelings that a sexual abuse victim have are just that - one of a victim. Why? Because you truly were a victim or a slave to someone else's will for your life in a short or long term period of time. Serving someone who has wounded or misused you can feel like punishment on top of pain. But God is asking us to serve Him through our service to others. The service of a bondservant is not just a one-time service, but a life-long commitment to Jesus Christ and others.

You will be a slave or a servant but none of us are free will agents with no master. ~Author Unknown

Many years ago while thinking about the things I had done prior to marriage to my minister/ missionary husband, I felt very sad for my actions. I truly believed when I asked Christ into my life that I wanted to be good, but just kept messing up. Becoming completely accountable to my husband after marriage was the ingredient in my life that I sincerely needed. When boxed in tightly, there was no longer physical room for error in my life. But my emotions and my past still weighed heavily upon my mind. I had actually said at one time that I would do what God told me to do even if it hurt. In my mind, to follow God would be harder and more painful than to live like the devil.

I knew that to follow God meant that I had to walk away from certain friends and habits that I had formed over my lifetime. To follow God meant that I could no longer do whatever I felt like but I had to do what was right according to the Word of God, His Bible. To follow God meant that I would have to apologize when I wanted to be apologized to. The list does continue. I had plenty of time to do my own thing by this stage of my life. My husband was my newly found accountability partner that I had not chosen -- God had chosen for me.

To obey God meant that I had to obey my husband also, for he was the one person who could tell me when I was wrong, with my permission of course, never rudely or hurtfully. No one likes to be told they are wrong, especially when we believe we are right. Habits that we form, traditions that we pick up from parents who were also wrong, ways of thinking that we declare to be true but are not, are all reasons for change. The hardest person to point out corrections for wrong behavior is someone who is convinced that they are right. I believed myself to be right the majority of the time and the rest of the world just needed to catch up with my wisdom. The thought of being wise did not really cross my mind; the need to be in control so that I would not be hurt was my problem. I was so caught up in the pain of the past and avoidance of rejection that my way was always the right way. So it goes for many others.

If you are now thinking, "Poor woman, I would never act like that!", then you are exactly the person who needs to hear my confession. You are the controlling person who sees yourself as the one who has no real problems; therefore, it is always others who have the problem. You are always the one who has to do for others, be for others, clean up behind others, change for others. Your victim mentality is the exact problem and the reason that you have a hard time with others. Being an actual victim and acting like a victim are very different. The reason "others" is your problem is because you have never looked at yourself as the common denominator of all your relationships. You are the one person who is in every relationship you have ever had; therefore, it is not others who are at fault in your relationships, it is you. There are times when it is truly others who are doing the wrong things, but mostly it is you.

God gave me a word back that I still share today. "Satan's freedom is bondage. Christ's bondage is freedom." When we follow our own feelings or desires, we are in bondage to Satan. Before becoming a Christian, it was easy to do the wrong thing because I did whatever I felt like doing. My feelings were in control; therefore, if I was in a bad mood, I let everyone know it and did not care if I treated someone harshly. I was "free to be me"! The problem came when I felt like doing something that I should not - I did it anyway because I was "free to be me and no one could make me do whatever I did not want to do!" "Don't tell me what to do!" is a statement of rebellion and disrespect for authority.

When we are our own authority, we will not allow anyone to have authority over us, including God. Therefore, to give in to Christ, to allow Him to be the Lord of my life and to use my husband to bring discipline back into my life meant that I had to give up "my freedom to be me" and become a bond slave to Him. What I found was that as I gave up my freedom to follow whatever my feelings and emotions dictated to me, I actually gained more freedom than I had ever known before. As I gave up my right to "be me", I became more like Christ over the years. There was less need to be in control and more desire to serve others. There was less need to make others do what I wanted and more freedom to let others be themselves when they were around me.

Please understand that as Christians we are not called to be doormats to be walked upon and over. We are called to be an example of Christ to this present world so that people will be drawn to God. Jesus made His share of people mad when He was on this earth, but His motives were based on love for people, not on getting His own way. To be Christ-like means that we must not demand our way but to serve others as God changes their hearts just as others served us as He changes ours.

24.) Are you willing to be a bondservant to Christ after you have discovered the meaning even though it means serving Him by serving others?

25.) **Read Matthew 21:21-22.** The immovable mountain in your life can be due to sexual abuse, acquired behaviors of self-protection, deep-rooted mistrust, shame and contempt, and a skewed view of God the Father, or a combination of any of these. Other than your past sexual abuse, are there any other parts of your life that you struggle with or are overwhelmed by?

26.) Are there parts of your sexual abuse that feel like a mountain on your shoulders and look too large to conquer? Explain your answer.

27.) Can you conquer this issue(s) even if your faith is the size of a mustard seed right now, which is the tiniest of seeds but grows into a large tree? How?

28.) **Read Matthew 17:18-21**.   In verse 19, what was the disciples' question? Write it out.

Verse 21 gives a special provision for a specific type of demon. There is extra effort that must be used to cast this demon out of the child. With certain mindsets caused by sexual abuse, we must make extra efforts to make these mindsets "go out". This can be as difficult as climbing the mountain instead of trying to remove it. We want to be rescued from our wounds. We want God to just make it go away. We want to forget it and leave it behind pretending that nothing is wrong in our lives. Fake it until you make it is good for some areas of our lives and devastating in others. Special care to overcome can lead to extra work on our parts to change our mindsets in order to have healing and peace restored to us.

29.) **Read Isaiah 41:8-16**. Summarize what verses 14-16 say about:

v. 14 You –

v. 14 God –

v. 15 God –

v. 15 You –

v. 16 You –

v. 16 Whom is your joy in?

30.) Who wants to conquer the mountain of your pain with you and for you?

31.) Does God want you to walk through your healing journey alone? Or does He choose to carry you through it as according to Isaiah 53:3-6? Explain your answer.

Jesus was born for a purpose as the Son of God, to die on the cross as a sacrifice for our sins. We too are created and born with a purpose for our lives. We are made to look the way we do with our specific hair, eye, skin color and body shape. We have the personality that we need to accomplish the tasks we were created to accomplish. We are a perfect and beautiful creation, created and loved by the same God who created the universe. He designed and formed you in your mother's womb and you are His precious possession.

32.) **Read and summarize Jeremiah 29:11.**

Dear God,

In Jesus' Name, Amen.

REMINDER: Please remember to Journal daily…

Chapter 5

Helpless and Hopeless

Who I Am In Christ

Read daily. Put your name in the blank.

The Word of God Says...

_________________ is the light of the world...Matthew 5:14

_________________ is part of the true vine...John 15:5

_________________ is Christ's friend...John 15:15

_________________ is a joint heir with Christ...Romans 8:17

_________________ is righteous and holy...Ephesians 4:24

_________________ is a child of light and not of darkness...1 Thessalonians 5:5

_________________ is an enemy of the devil...1 Peter 5:8

_________________ is a slave of righteousness...Romans 6:18

_________________ is enslaved to God...Romans 6:22

_________________ is born of God, and the evil one – the devil – cannot touch me.
1 John 5:18

Objective:

- Analyze an historical account of a woman who was sexually abused.
- Explore personal experiences of sexual abuse and feelings associated with the episodes.
- Realize and accept God's love.
- Change feelings of hopelessness to feelings of success.

Inspiration:

> Jeremiah 29:11 (NKJV) *"For I know the thoughts that I think toward you, thoughts of peace and not evil, says the the Lord, to give you a future and a hope.*

The Journey Continues... 

Helpless

I want to tell you the story of a 15 year old black girl who had been sent to live with a white couple and their young daughter

The man of the house, Dr. James Norcom, immediately began to make sexual advances on the girl. Although his wife was suspicious, she did nothing to help her out of her situation.

Over time, Dr. Norcom moved the girl out of his home away from his wife, into another house to insure private sexual advances on his victim. Eventually, he violently refused to allow her to marry a young black man that she had fallen in love with.

Out of rebellion, she became involved with a single white lawyer, became pregnant and, in the hope that her guardian would become so angry that he would allow her to leave his care, she gave birth to the child.

Although infuriated, he would not stop his sexual advances nor would he let her leave, so she continued the illicit affair with her white lover, giving birth to a second child. After having her second child she stated, "it was something to triumph over my tyrant in that small way".

After seven years of abuse by this man, she learned that he had plans to take her children away from her. Finally, she had had enough and ran away from home.

Out of fear of being found by Dr. Norcom, she moved from house to house, staying with neighbors until the white father was able to get custody of their children.

Knowing that her children were finally safe she made a decision that would change her life, just so she could remain close to the children that she loved in spite of her years of heartache. She moved into a tiny crawlspace above a porch in her grandmother and uncle's house. The space was nine feet long and seven feet wide. Its sloped ceiling was only three feet high at one end and didn't allow her to turn while lying down without hitting her shoulder. Rats and mice crawled over her; there was no light and no ventilation. Her children were now living in the same house. She could even see them while they played outside through a peephole she had drilled. She lived in the crawlspace for seven years, coming out only for brief periods at night for exercise. She had now endured 14 years of abuse and maltreatment. She was 29 years old.

You may ask, "Did this just happen?" "How could a doctor be so cruel? Someone should lock him up." "Wait until the ACLU gets wind of this one."

The person was Harriet Tubman, and in 1842, she made escape to freedom. Later she earned the name "Moses" for helping to free 300 slaves, in 19 trips with the Underground Railroad. Two of those slaves were her 70 year old parents.

Her tactic? She not only outwitted the white men who were after the $40,000 price on her head, but she carried a gun which she used to threaten the fugitives if they became too tired or decided to turn back, telling them, "You'll be free or die." She never lost a single person.

Perhaps you may be thinking that she was older, braver, had more or less to lose than you do or did. Harriet Tubman was one of the greater women of our time, a true inspiration and hero to the helpless. Even if you do not see yourself as courageous as she was, there is a change in the way you see yourself that _can_ greatly improve _your_ vision of you.

Just like Harriet Tubman, a sexual abuser can silently take away your ability to help yourself or save yourself. The power that they have in your life is overwhelming to the point of frozen fear. Do we dare turn to the right or the left? Harriet was on her back in a crawlspace, unable to turn to the right or the left, for seven years, due to fear of one man. Breaking the cycle of fear and helplessness is the only way to come out of the crawlspace that has become a mental prison to you. Seeing yourself as capable and helped by God will give you the courage that it takes to defeat the enemies of your past and your happiness. Renewing your mind and letting go of the old image of you is necessary in the change process.

Gideon: What is your self-image?

In Judges, there is a story of a young man named Gideon who did not think of himself as great at all. But with the help of God, renewing his self-image from one of hiding and fear to one of going to battle and defeating his enemy, he was able to give his entire family, as well as himself, freedom.

Read Judges 6:1-16

In verse 11, Gideon, the youngest son, is still at home doing everyday tasks, but hiding from his enemies while he is doing it. He is not out in the open where wheat threshing occurs so the wind can carry away the chaff (hulls) to separate it from the fruit (seed).

In verse 12, the Angel of the Lord points out Gideon's potential. Although he is hiding just as the rest of Israel is hiding in the mountains in verse 2, he is still brave enough to continue to try and save some of the grain for his own family.

1.) When you feel the enemy (your memories, every day reminders, seeing certain people) coming into your mind and causing stress, what do you do? Explain.

2.) At the time of your sexual abuse, even if you were very young, did you feel as though you wanted to run to the mountains and hide in a cave? Explain.

3.) Write out Jeremiah 29:11.

4.) After abuse stops or during abuse, many feel as though God has abandoned them. We feel that for some unknown reason, we are not like the rest of the world who are worthy of protection and happiness. According to Jeremiah, God still has a good life planned for us. The concept of a good plan and purpose verses experiences of sexual abuse does not make sense to many. Why not?

5.) **Reread Judges 6:13**. What did Gideon say to the Lord in this verse?

If the Lord –

Why has –

And where are –

But now –

Reread verse 14. God's response back to Gideon's questions and accusation was to remind Gideon of who he really is in spite of the way his life seemed to be. God said to Gideon to "go in this your", what? Your might. What kind of might was God telling him? Not the might of his own strength and will but in the strength and will of the fact that God told him to go. If he would just make a move in the direction that God told him to go, he would defeat his enemy.

6.) Instead in verse 15, Gideon disregarded what God said his purpose in life was and focused on the complete helplessness he felt. What did he say to the Lord to prove how lowly and unworthy he felt he was in his own eyes and in his opinion of his family and peers?

God knew Gideon and his family better than Gideon. He had created them. But Gideon was so caught up in his present circumstance that he had forgotten his true identity. Let's look at the reality of Gideon's family history that created a warrior, not a coward.

In Genesis 41:51 we discover that Manasseh was actually Joseph's oldest son. The eldest son has the first birthright and is heir to all the father has.

In Genesis 48:17-19 we discover that even though Manasseh is the oldest and expects the blessings of his father Joseph and his grandfather Jacob, Ephraim, his younger brother and second born receives the blessing from his grandfather Jacob.

Because Jacob, his grandfather, blessed Ephraim, the youngest, in spite of Joseph's protest, and Joseph blessed his oldest son Manasseh at the time of his death, there is a family problem - favoritism at its finest. Manasseh had every right to be angry and resentful of what his grandfather had done to him by splitting his inheritance, but he was not.

In Numbers 32, Joshua 13:29-33, and Joshua 14:2-4 we are able to see that Moses was able to settle the problem peaceably, with the cooperation of everyone involved. When the twelve tribes of Israel came to the Promised Land, half of the tribe of Manasseh decided that they would prefer to stay on the east side of the Jordan River, where Gideon now resides as their descendant. The other half of the tribe of Manasseh and the tribe of Ephraim crossed over into the Promised Land and took possession of their father, Joseph's, portion of the land.

Gideon's descendant came from a line of high rank in Israel; he was one of the twelve tribes of Israel through Joseph. Gideon's forefathers, who settled in the land east of the Jordan, were Manasseh and his son Machir. They were great warriors.

His heritage was rich, but like Benjamin (I Samuel 9:21) and King David, he was the youngest in his family and now God was calling him to action in order to save his entire family. God saw in these young men something that they and their families did not see, the ability to fight when the time was right and the ability to lead when it was time to lead.

7.) Have you ever felt that God was asking you to do something, and your response was to tell Him all that was wrong with you? What did He tell you to do?

8.) What was it that you told Him about yourself, both positives and negatives?

     Caught in the Act of Grace Women's Bible Study

9.) Gideon's protest did not change God's declaration. Verse 16 shows the Lord's response. Write out His words in verse 16.

Now rewrite the verse using your own name in place of the references to Gideon.

Hopelessness

There are times in everyone's life that despair and hopelessness seem to come over and settle on us like a heavy blanket. The weight is there and the comfort of not being exposed is there, but the desire to hide is not what we really want. We want hope for a good future. We search everywhere, running to anything, accepting whatever is told to us, in an effort to find something that will make the world we know feel right again.

One of those days occurred and I found it stretching into weeks. The hopelessness that I felt for change to happen in my life swallowed me whole. All I wanted to do was write, but could not, and I cared about nothing else. Sitting on my porch on a sunny afternoon, I heard a drop that sounded strange. There had been no rain and it was late in the day. Why the drip was happening led me on a search. I saw it was coming from under the eave of my house, so going upstairs and crawling out the window of my son's bedroom, I went to the point of origin of the drip. Not finding a reason still, I decided to go back inside. I looked around at the view of my surroundings from this angle on top of my house. My family thought it was very comical when I told them what I had done.

I sat on the roof, in the shade next to the chimney, in my robe and house shoes, for an hour and a half, absorbing the sights and sounds of the woods in front of me. The peace of it all was wonderful, and the giggle of what someone would think if they drove up, made a joy bubble up inside of me.

While sitting on my roof, I allowed my mind to also drift through my life and relationships, and a story formed that expressed my past hopelessness better than I could ever explain.

The Woods of Hope
by Darla Weaver

The trees were green and swaying as a squirrel raced from treetop to treetop. The path he followed was well known and sure, as he scurried form branch to branch. No need to look down from the treetop racetrack that he ran on, for falling was never going to happen. He was built and ready to live in the windy world of pine needles and acorns from the mighty plants made of wood. He knew what he wanted and knew how to get it. Willingly indignant at any insistence that his home could belong to anyone but him. Nowhere is there a treetop warrior more ready to protect than here, for what belongs to him is his alone.

All around the squirrel's tree were other sounds beginning to take shape. Woodpeckers were digging out their dinner from under dead bark. Insects can never be hidden from these professional exterminators, for they are built to retrieve. Small finches twerp out their dances among the bushes close to the ground. How much fun they all seem to have, snapping seeds off the ground in a relentless game of tag.

Buzzards soar high in the sky, lazily drifting as they decide where to roost for the evening. Forever circling and circling, watching for a possible meal, hoping that soon something will die. When the end of one life comes, the continuation of another is catapulted for the time being into the blissful satisfaction of a full stomach.

What is lurking under the leaves on the ground, around the other edge of the forest, past the skyline? Nearby sleeping frogs, snakes and bugs, buried deep in the ground, wait for the earth to warm around them indicating that Spring has arrived. But what is out there just a little further? Hope!

Hope is the fleeting, white image of something that is tangible, but not hold-able. It is a gift given, but easily snatched away. The desire to grasp the shimmering image can be overwhelming. The desire to be loved and wanted, only to be dashed against the sharp and protruding rocks of unheard longing. Where does it all end, but then again, where did it start? Hope, once lost, can it be found?

What if hope were a little dog lost in the woods? Would someone come and find her before a wild animal devours her. Would anyone care that she is missing? How long would it take to discover that the curiosity that led her into the woods to start with, would also be her undoing. There is no hope when all the world looks the same and directions become confused. What is north, or south, or east or west? When a sound travels, the distortion of the trees makes it impossible to know which direction to walk.

Confusion and panic fill the little dog called Hope. She stops to see if her master is coming, but is unsure of where to go. The smells of this world are different, and she is unwanted at every bend in this road that she unwittingly has stumbled into. The warmth she believed was hers forever has now turned into the cold and steely reality of no more.

Hope is gone; the forever circling buzzard sits back with the satisfaction of a full stomach.

My family's first response to the rooftop story was, "Wow, you killed off the little dog?" My husband even teared up at the thought of my feelings. The depth of my pain became reality to him for the first time. Even as a Christian, the loneliness that had been in me was deep and wide. God was always there, always comforting me, keeping me in love with Him and I never wanted to disappoint Him with my actions and words. It was people who had my thoughts captured.

Hope lost is a terrible thing, hope regained is a reward beyond measure. The comfort of knowing that your feelings are shared by others is refreshing. But the loss of hope is not where anyone can live for very long. God has a better plan for us. He wants to save us, love us, provide for us, keep us close to Him and give us the choice to allow Him to do all of these things for us. Hope is never gone; it is only sometimes delayed until we are willing to receive it. God never leaves us lost in a world willing to devour us, if we reach up to Him and allow Him to lead us to a safe place. The fear of the unknown can render us immovable in the direction of changing the way we act and think, the people we hang out with, and the places we go. In the end, it is our decision to live the miserable life we have always lived or to have the abundant life that God wants to give us.

                    Caught in the Act of Grace Women's Bible Study

King David: What did I do to deserve this?

In 1 Samuel 16:11-13, David was anointed to be King of Israel by the prophet Samuel after Saul sinned against God and continued in rebellion. Even though David was a youth when anointed, from that day forward the Spirit of the Lord began to prepare David to be king. But, before he could be king, he had to see himself as king and believe God would give him the wisdom and ability to lead His people. David did not seek to be king; God declared him King of Israel.

10.) **Read Matthew 3:16–17**. When John the Baptist baptized Jesus, did Jesus or John declare Jesus "His Son" or did God?

11.) Did you ask to be born in this time, to this family, and live this life, or did God appoint you (or create you) to live in these times?

12.) **Read 1 Samuel 18:1-12**. In verse 1 and 2, was David born into Saul's family or was he placed in Saul's family as an "adopted" son by Saul?

13.) Although Jonathon is the firstborn son of Saul and should inherit the birthright of the firstborn, he gave his birthright to David. What is it about David that made Jonathon desire to submit to him? (The answer is found in 1 Samuel 16:18)

14.) **Read 1 Samuel 18:1-9**. What did David do to receive such anger from Saul?

15.) **Read 1 Samuel 18:10-12**. As usual, when David knew that Saul was troubled, David came to him to sing and soothe Saul. This time when David came into the room, Saul threw a spear at him to kill him (verse 11). Many times when we have tried to be kind to others, the result is something bad may happen to us or we are hurt in some way. Is there a time when you have been kind but harshness returned? Explain.

16.) At the time that you were sexually abused, were you doing your normal routine in life, whether a child or adult, and someone "threw a spear at you"? Explain

When direct assault did not work, I Samuel 18:10-21 states Saul tried another tactic at destroying David. He uses the love his daughter has for David to wound him. Although Michal loves David dearly, she does turn out to be a treacherous wife to David. She is her father's daughter and David's wound is very personal now.

Read I Samuel 19:1-7. David's relationship with Jonathon, his brother-in-law, is one of brotherhood, affection and servitude in which Jonathon warns David of Saul's next plot to kill him.

17.) At this point in David's life, what do you think he may be thinking about himself and his life?

18.) Do you believe David deserves the treatment that he is getting?

19.) Why is his father-in-law abusing him?

20.) Why does Jonathon have to continue to step in to protect David from his father?

21.) After all of these things "continue to happen" to David in his life, he still remains faithful and positive toward God and the life that God says he will have someday as king. In your life, do you believe that you have remained as positive as David has?

If not, what can you do to get a positive attitude renewed in your life at this point? I don't know is not an appropriate answer.

What Did I Do Wrong?

Finally, read **1 Samuel 20**. In verses 1-4, David finally asks Jonathan the questions; "Why?", "What have I done?", "What is my wickedness?", and "What is my sin before your father?"

22.) Have you asked yourself these same questions about your sexual abuse and your family situation growing up?

23.) Did David do anything to deserve Saul's cruelty?

24.) Did you do anything to deserve the pain that you have been through?

If you believe the answer is yes or maybe, please read John 3:16-21. God loves you so much that He was willing to let His Son die for you, to forgive you of your sins and not to judge you harshly. In judging ourselves without mercy, we are saying that we are not worthy of forgiveness and Jesus' death on the cross was for nothing. Our sin is un-forgiveness of ourselves and self-condemnation. When we condemn ourselves, we become without hope of ever having joy even in the best of times. Jesus wants to expose our sin without shaming us in our sin. He was willing to pay the ultimate price for you.

25.) Are you willing to allow His act of love to replace the act of pain that someone else caused and allow yourself to be rescued out of your pit of hopeless condemnation?

In answering yes, this time there is freedom, not imprisonment. In answering yes, you are allowing yourself to cut the silent chains that have held you bound. In answering yes, you are now allowing others to begin the journey into your old world of self-preservation through isolation. The loneliness that haunts you in the middle of a crowd can now begin the descent out of you and the joy of the Lord can begin the ascent into you.

Matthew Henry's Bible Commentary says this about 1 Samuel 20:41-42:

> "the most sorrowful paring of these two friends, who, for aught that appears, never came together again but once, and that was by stealth in a wood, 1 Samuel 23:16. 1) David addressed himself to Jonathon with the reverence of a servant rather than the freedom of a

friend: He fell on his face to the ground, and bowed himself three times, as one deeply sensible of his obligations to him for the good services he had done him. 2) They took leave of each other with the greatest affection imaginable, with kisses and tears; they wept on each other's neck till David wept the most <u>Samuel 20:41.</u> The separation of two such faithful friends was equally grievous to them both, but David's case was the more deplorable; for, when Jonathan was returning to his family and friends, David was leaving all his comforts, even those of God's sanctuary, and therefore his grief exceeded Jonathan's, or perhaps it was because his temper was more tender and his passions were stronger. 3) They referred themselves to the covenant of friendship that was between them, both of them comforting themselves with this in this mournful separation: "We have sworn both of us in the name of the Lord, for ourselves and our heirs, that we and they will be faithful and kind to each other from generation to generation." Thus, while we are at home in the body and absent from the Lord, this is our comfort, that he has made with us an everlasting covenant."

The sorrow that David felt, at being the one who was brought into the family through no effort of his own, then the one cast out of the family for no cause of his own, was heartbreaking for him. He left everything that he knew and went into the wilderness to live, hunted by Saul all the while. Even those who helped David were killed by Saul. At this point in life, it would be acceptable for most if David gave up and gave in to the pitiful circumstances that he continued to find himself in. Except for one thing, Samuel, God's prophet, anointed him King. And Nathan, God's prophet, relays God's covenant to David, 2 Samuel 7:1-17. David was "A man after God's own heart."

We are daughters and sons of the King, bought with a price and sealed by the blood of the Cross of Calvary. Once we give ourselves to Jesus, He never throws us away like trash. We are His and He loves us just the way we are; bumps, bruises, scars and all. We are safe and loved.

Where was God in the midst of your abuse? Did He see what was happening to you? Did He see you doing things that in your heart you knew were wrong? Do you hide your face in shame of the memories? Do you refuse to think about them because these things happened so long ago?

We cry out in our thoughts or say out loud, "God, where are you, why don't you make this go away?"

The practical side of life is that God gave us a soul and a mind. When our soul is wounded, the mind remembers. Memories never leave us. Even the diseased mind of an Alzheimer's patient remembers certain things all the way to the end of their life. To ask for memories to leave us is to ask God to give us holes in our past. The ones who do have holes in their past pray and ask God to help the memories to return. Every event that takes place in our life time is stored in a magnificent work of art called the brain. Mental pictures of smiling faces, pleasant vacations, beautiful flowers, sleeping babies and hard won victories are all mixed in with wounding words, sexual abuse, failures, punches to the face and conditional love.

                                    Caught in the Act of Grace Women's Bible Study

To remove a memory is impossible. To change the pattern of thinking is not. To continue to rehearse a healed and forgiven past in our minds will only keep the wound alive and active. To replace the memory, actively change the memory to a positive one. This can take place only after the acceptance and forgiveness toward the person or situation that caused negative feelings to emerge is completed. When the thoughts of your past pop into your mind, you now have the ability to say, "God has delivered me from that and I don't have to take it back by thinking on it. It is a part of my past and I accept that, but it is only useful to my future if it gives hope of healing to someone who needs to hear my testimony!"

Below is how.

Philippians 4:6-9 (AMP) *"Do not fret or have any anxiety about anything, but in every circumstance and in everything, by prayer and petition (definite requests), with thanksgiving, continue to make your wants known to God. 7) And God's peace [shall be yours, that tranquil state of a soul assured of its salvation through Christ, and so fearing nothing from God and being content with its earthly lot of whatever sort that is, that peace] which transcends all understanding shall garrison and mount guard over your hearts and minds in Christ Jesus. 8) For the rest, brethren, whatever is true, whatever is worthy of reverence and is honorable and seemly, whatever is just, whatever is pure, whatever is lovely and lovable, whatever is kind and winsome and gracious, if there is any virtue and excellence, if there is anything worthy of praise, think on and weigh and take account of these things [fix your minds on them]. 9) Practice what you have learned and received and heard and seen in me, and model your way of living on it, and the God of peace (of untroubled, undisturbed well-being) will be with you."*

Ephesians 4:22-24 (AMP) *"Strip yourselves of your former nature [put off and discard your old un-renewed self] which characterized your previous manner of life and becomes corrupt through lusts and desires that spring from delusion; 23) And be constantly renewed in the spirit of your mind [having a fresh mental and spiritual attitude], (24) And put on the new nature (the regenerate self) created in God's image, [Godlike] in true righteousness and holiness."*

Romans 12:2 (AMP) *"Do not be conformed to this world (this age), [fashioned after and adapted to its external, superficial customs], but be transformed (changed) by the [entire] renewal of your mind [by its new ideals and its new attitude], so that you may prove [for yourselves] what is the good and acceptable and perfect will of God, even the thing which is good and acceptable and perfect [in His sight for you]."*

God was with you from the moment that He decided to create you. He has never left your side although He will allow you to have a free will to decide what you want to do with your life.

Use the verses in Philippians, Ephesians, and Romans as an inspiration for your prayer. Change your mindset from helpless and hopeless to conquering and hope-filled.

Prayer:

Dear Lord:

In Jesus' Name, Amen.

Remider: Please remember to Journal daily…

Chapter 6

The Ambivalent Relationship

Who I Am In Christ

Read daily. Put your name in the blank.

The Word of God Says...

_________________ is saved...1 Thessalonians 5:9; Titus 3:5; Hebrews 7:25

_________________ is redeemed...1 Peter 1:18-19; Galatians 3:13

_________________ is strong to the end...1 Corinthians 1:8

_________________ is near to Jesus...Ephesians 2:13

_________________ is set free...John 8:31-32

_________________ is more than a conqueror...Romans 8:37

_________________ is sealed with the Holy Spirit...Ephesians 1:13

_________________ is in Jesus Christ...1 Corinthians 1:30

_________________ is complete in Him...Colossians 2:10

_________________ is free from condemnation...Romans 8:1

Objective:

- Learn that past relationship incapability does not mean you will have present relationship incapability.
- For married people, physical touch is necessary and enjoyable.
- Jesus never left you, even at the time of the abuse.
- Molestation does not lead to homosexuality.

Inspiration:

Luke 16:13 (NKJV) *"No servant can serve two masters; for either he will hate the one and love the other, or else he will be loyal to the one and despise the other. You cannot serve God and mammon."*

The Journey Continues...

What is Ambivalence?

Luke 16:13 (NKJV) King David has lived a life that has been very revealing in all areas that we live in today. After the rape of his daughter, Tamar, her brother Absalom began a campaign of revenge on his father. Because King David has not acted decisively with any of his three oldest children, he had much to regret with their rearing. Tamar was devastated. Amnon was dead. And now Absalom had stolen his throne. King David had made up his mind that he would not fight against Absalom no matter what happened, hoping that someday things would be right again. David loved his son. He would rather have given up his throne than had anything to happen to Absalom, no matter how he behaved. Over time and many battles, Absalom died. David's humiliation, grief, love for his children, unwillingness to fight for his own throne or his own reputation caused ambivalent feelings toward Absalom. Once he was dead, the people were left without knowing what to do. Do they trust that the king will not allow his love for his son to dominate his decisions? Or do they hope that the king will see Absalom as the enemy that he was? Joab made David face his feelings and make things right with the people.

2 Samuel 19:4-6 *"But the king covered his face, and the king cried out with a loud voice, "O my son Absalom! O Absalom, my son, my son!" Then Joab came into the house to the king, and said, "Today you have disgraced all your servants who today have saved your life, the lives of your sons and daughters, the lives of your wives and the lives of your concubines, in that you love your enemies and hate your friends. For you have declared today that you regard neither princes nor servants; for today I perceive that if Absalom had lived and all of us had died today, then it would have pleased you well."*

Ambivalence, what in the world does that mean! That was the thought I had the first time I ever read the word. It wasn't even in my computer's dictionary. So, did someone just make it up to cause me grief? Actually, one Google search gave me the definition, and it made complete sense.

Ambivalence - having two opposing emotions occurring at the same time, like love and hate, shame and contempt, or desire and disgust.

Being in a confused state of feeling, and understanding two emotions at the same instant can be hard to identify, much less understand. For instance, a parent or sibling molested you and you intensely hate that part of them, but at the same time you intensely love them because they are your parents or sibling. The split in the emotional part of you might even feel like a split in your personality. "Who are you today?" may be the question you ask yourself every time you are around that person. "Am I the person who loves you or the person who hates you? Can I trust you to be true to the emotion that I feel right now?"

I don't really enjoy Chinese food anymore. There was a time when I did like it. My husband took us to eat at a Chinese restaurant every single Sunday for over one year. After biting into ingredients that I couldn't identify, but was too mannerly to spit out of my mouth, I no longer eat it unless I must. When I do go to a Chinese restaurant there are two things that I know I like to eat, rice and Sweet and Sour Chicken. My favorite part of this dish, besides being able to identify everything on my plate, is the sauce. Sweet and sour is a strange combination of tastes being mixed into one experience.

Ambivalence is a strange combination of emotions, all mixed into one experience. The emotions are not what you question at all, they are just fact. Feelings are neither right nor wrong, they are just feelings. What it questions is the normalcy of feeling them. Are there other people who feel this? Do I have a split personality, is there something wrong with me? Am I scared to admit what I am feeling for fear of being thought mentally unstable, and can I get over how I feel? The list of questions can go on and on. Obtaining and maintaining a sense of direction, in the feeling that is felt toward a certain person, can often feel like groping in the dark for a light switch in a room that is unfamiliar.

One Woman's Story

One particular woman was molested by her brother. Because he was a step brother and she was in her late childhood and early teens, she felt a large amount of responsibility. Although she never wanted the abuse to happen, she did not refuse it. The exchange from him that she received was being invited to "hang out with him and his friends". None of the other siblings were invited.

At the same time the step brother was molesting her, his younger sister was also molesting this woman's little brother. The two older step children were separately molesting the younger step children. To add to her distress, she knew what was happening to her little brother and did not tell in that case either for fear of losing her big brother's "love". As she grew, this "love" was no longer tolerated and the shame that she felt earlier began to deepen dramatically. Once she grew up and was married with children of her own, the "love" she grew up understanding was transferred to her husband. Therefore, she never understood why she could never trust her husband's love for her, nor could she believe that he only loved her simply because he loved her. She believed there had to be a hidden motive and she was there to be used by him. The transference of her brother's "love" continued in her self-worth, how she parented her children, and how she related to people on every level.

Her relationship with her older brother stayed exactly the same. She did not tell on him, and she never expressed any disdain toward him; she really did love and admire him as her older brother. All of this continued into her 40's. Because this emotional lifestyle was so ingrained into her for 30 years, she could no longer distinguish between love and hate, shame and contempt, and right and wrong emotions toward anyone, including her husband and her own two children. The confusion of not knowing how she should feel toward her husband and children versus how she could not feel added to her shame. She was completely convinced that the molestation of herself and her little brother was all her fault and the step sibling had little to do with it.

The blame that the victim can take on herself is usually tremendous, and in this case she felt an incredible need to protect her abusive brother from retribution as an adult for acts that he committed as a teenager. She was willing to sacrifice her relationship with her husband and the inappropriate bonding that she had with her young children who were now refusing to obey her.

Another Woman's Story

In another case, the woman had been molested the first ten years of her life, and had no memory of anytime she was not being molested by someone. The molesters were numerous and of all ages. The confusion in her emotions did not come from the molesters. She knew that they were wrong in what they did, and she was willing to forgive them over time and with much effort. The ambivalent emotions that she had were toward her mother. She had wanted her mother to protect her when she was small, but she never told her mother what was happening to her. The mother never suspected that the little girl was being abused in spite of tending the wounds left by the abusers. The mother's own set of issues bled into her relationship with her daughter and a shame/contempt relationship was established. For 39 years the child had tried to win the affection of her mother, but for those same years the mother pushed her away when the daughter got too close to her.

The abuse from early childhood, starting around the age of three or earlier, had set the little girl up for a shame/contempt view of relationships, and the mother reinforced her pattern. Her life with her husband, two children, and every friend that she ever made was based on the assumption that once they knew her, they would shame her, feel contempt for her, or reject her. Because of this attitude, she set up every relationship for failure and was never disappointed. This confirmed that she really was the bad person she felt she was, and was as unlovable as her mother had taught her. Her husband was the secondary victim; he received all of the retribution from her past. The shame that her abusers made her feel, followed by the contempt that her mother had for her, mixed together in her attitude toward people and herself, caused distorted emotions.

Relationships of the past do affect relationships today.

Both of these women have very clear shame/contempt emotions toward themselves as well as extreme love/contempt emotions toward others. As the saying goes, "You can't see the forest for the trees". They both had to face and accept their feelings and allow the responsible parties to have responsibility for their actions, before healing and healthy relationships could be established with anyone. This was a very rewarding accomplishment for them both, but the hard work of changing how they viewed themselves and others had been established. Their main healing came in the form of value they achieved for themselves, and for the first time in their lives, they became more important than the value they had believed others had for them.

1.) How can an ambivalent relationship be identified? Write out how someone close to you makes you feel the majority of the time. This includes the desire to protect them more than protecting yourself

2.) Do you recognize dual feelings toward them? Perhaps you must put your trust in them but you don't trust them not to hurt you deeply. (How to trust and not trust?)

3.) If you were to have an honest conversation with this person about how they make you feel, what would you say to them? Write out your answer.

4.) Do you believe that your protection of them is more important than your protection of yourself, perhaps even more important than protecting the wounded little girl inside of you who really needs to be protected?

We must understand what is right about ourselves before we can face what is wrong about ourselves. For our entire lives we have valued ourselves very little, and victimization has always been our expectation. The thought that may come to mind when placed in uncomfortable situations is an automatic, "here we go again"; "why does this always keep happening?", "I deserve everything that this person is dishing out,"; "go ahead and be mean because I deserve it". These responses are wrong, and if someone were saying these things about themselves to you, you would readily reprimand them and build them back up. So why do you not do the same for yourself?

5.) What are your negative remarks that you use on yourself? For example: I'm just not good enough, or why should I expect anything good to happen to me when it never does?

6.) If someone you cared for said this to you about themselves, how would you respond to them?

  Caught in the Act of Grace Women's Bible Study

7.) Write out things you are good at, i.e. sports, decorating, business, gardening, hospitality, etc…

8.) Right now you are probably thinking, I see this on paper, but I don't feel it in my heart. What ambivalent emotions do you feel right now? i.e. I am good/bad, I am deserving/undeserving, I am willing/unwilling.

Jesus felt this same ambivalence when He was praying in the garden. The human side of Him did not want to go to the cross. He knew he would suffer tremendous torture and die. But, He willingly obeyed His Father and gave up His life for you and me. Therefore the cross is viewed with both shame and grace at the same time. Follow the sequence of events that Jesus went through.

Mark 14:22-25 (AMP) *"And while they were eating, He took a loaf [of bread], praised God and gave thanks and asked Him to bless it to their use. [Then] He broke [it] and gave to them and said, Take. Eat. This is My body. (23) He also took a cup [of the juice of grapes], and when He had given thanks, He gave [it] to them, and they all drank of it. (24) And He said to them, This is my blood [which ratifies] the new covenant, [the blood] which is being poured out for (on account of) many." [Exodus 24:8] (25) "Solemnly and sure I tell you, I shall not again drink of the fruit of the vine till that day when I drink of a new and a higher quality in God's kingdom."*

Mark 14:34-36 (AMP) *"And He said to them, My soul is exceedingly sad (overwhelmed with grief) so that it almost kills Me! Remain here and keep away and be watching. (35) And going a little farther, He fell on the ground and kept praying that if it were possible the [fatal] hour might pass from Him. (36) And He was saying, Abba, [which means] Father, everything is possible for You. Take away this cup from Me; yet not what I will, but what You [will]."*

Mark 15:33-34 (AMP) *"And when the sixth hour (about midday) had come, there was darkness over the whole land until the ninth hour (about three o'clock). (34) And at the ninth hour Jesus cried with a loud voice, Eloi, Eloi, lama sabachthani?—which means, My God, My God, why have You forsaken Me [deserting Me and leaving Me helpless and abandoned]?"* [Psalm 22:1.]

Hebrews 6:6 (AMP) *"If they then deviate from the faith and turn away from their allegiance—[it is impossible] to bring them back to repentance, for (because, while, as long as) they nail upon the cross the Son of God afresh [as far as they are concerned] and are holding [Him] up to contempt and shame and public disgrace."*

Hebrews 12:2 (AMP) *"Looking away [from all that will distract] to Jesus, Who is the Leader and the Source of our faith [giving the first incentive for our believe] and is also its Finisher [bringing it to maturity and perfection]. He, for the joy [of obtaining the prize] that was set before Him, endured the cross, despising and ignoring the shame, and is now seated at the right hand of the throne of God."* [Psalm 110:1.]

9.) Can you identify with the anticipation and pain that Jesus felt before He went to the cross when you think of encounters you have had with certain people?

10.) Have you felt shame and contempt, followed by a sense of abandonment and rejection (public disgrace) from people in your life? Even when you did nothing to deserve it? Explain your answers.

11.) What do you think Jesus did to overcome His fears and dread?

12.) What can you do to overcome your fears and dread?

13.) If Jesus died so you do not have the deep sense of aloneness and isolation, you must now accept that He is with you every second of every day. He puts great value on you and in you or He would never have died for you. Now that you know that Jesus Christ Himself has had the exact same emotions that you have, how do you feel?

14.) It makes no difference to God what you have done in your past; He loves you just the way you are. He would not have created you in the first place if He did not want you to have a good life filled with joy in knowing Him and knowing that He loves you. Love at this level is scary, especially if the "love" you have known has harmed you. Explain the difference between the love that you know and the love that God has for you. Be specific. Refer to "Who I am in Christ" if you are having difficulty knowing what to say.

  Caught in the Act of Grace Women's Bible Study

For Married Participants Only. If you are single, please skip to question 21.

Sexual Relationships with Your Spouse

The reference to love can also be confusing if your emotions are based on same sex molestation and physical responses. In creating man and woman in Genesis 2, God intended for the couple to procreate. Therefore, in the wondrous making of our bodies, He placed nerve endings in specific areas of our bodies to encourage the procreation process and to make us desire to touch one another. This touching and responding of our sexual organs was not only made by God but is encouraged by God. He wants us to enjoy each other physically. It is only in the abuse of this touching, by others or ourselves, that we lose sight of what God wants for us. Inappropriate attitudes toward sex (sex outside of a marriage bond or homosexual sex) and exposure to sex before we are mentally mature enough to fully understand it (childhood molestation) makes for a bad set up toward sexual identity.

God created us with certain sensations that involuntarily respond to stimuli. Not that there is any excuse for misuse of another human being, we are also not to condemn ourselves for the pleasure that is felt in the midst of an action that also disgusts us. The response of our bodies, due to contact with another, leads to further confusion, though we tell ourselves it was wrong. "If I didn't like the way I felt when he touched me, then I would not feel responsible." This same stimulus occurs in the marriage bed. The husband reaches out to touch his wife, a flashback to a memory of the past happens, she stiffens and he feels like she does not want anything to do with him.

Contrary to what a victim has learned about sexual relationships, the sense of dirtiness and distain, God's intent for sex was pure and lovely. Love and relationship is good and must be celebrated, not avoided and hated. In the Song of Solomon the Bible includes the most explicit account of a relationship between a man and woman, so that we will know completely the goodness and pureness of this kind of love.

Song of Solomon 2:2-7 (AMP) *"But Solomon replied, 'Like the lily among thorns, so are you, my love, among the daughters. (3) Like an apple tree among the trees of the wood, so is my beloved [shepherd] among the sons [cried the girl]? Under his shadow I delighted to sit, and his fruit was sweet to my taste. (4) He brought me to the banqueting house, and his banner over me was love [for love waved as a protecting and comforting banner over my head when I was near him]. (5) Sustain me with raisins; refresh me with apples, for I am sick with love. (6) [I can feel] his left hand under my head and his right hand embraces me!"* [Deuteronomy 33:27; Matthew 28:20.] *97) [He said] I charge you, O you daughters of Jerusalem, by the gazelles or by the hinds of the field [which are free to follow their own instincts] that you not try to stir up or awaken [my] love until it pleases."*

15.) After reading these five verses in the Song of Solomon from the Old Testament, what is your first reaction to these verses?

16.) The sexual references in these verses are not pornographic by any means, and neither has the devil been allowed to make the person writing them feel nasty. But, because of our experiences with sex in the past, we have a distorted view and nasty memories. How do you think you can come to the place in your own thinking, of having the same attitude toward a lover as this person?

17.) Did it ever occur to you that God made sex? He approves of sex and He wants you to use sex with your spouse as a means of celebrating each other and Him.

18.) The result of sex is the creation of a child, whom many refer to as "evidence of the love two people have for each other". What does that phrase mean to you?

19.) When Adam and Eve ate the apple in the Garden of Eden, sin entered the world. Because sin is always there, evil cannot be avoided. But, even before sin entered, God had a plan that included Adam and Eve having sex. Why do you think God intended this for them?

20.) If Jesus lives in your heart and you are a Christian, then you also claim that He is with you all of the time. All of the time means that He is there with you, even when you are intimate with your spouse. Has the thought ever occurred to you that when you are intimate, Jesus is there watching over you in approval? **Reread Song of Solomon 2:4.**

Jesus Is With You all the Time.

21.) He was with you at the exact time of your abuse. Even though something very evil was happening to you, you were not the only one there being abused. Jesus was right there with you. **Read Isaiah 53: 3-4.** How was Jesus treated in the first part of verse 3?

22.) Is He familiar with all of the pain and humiliation you have endured? See verse 3.

1 Peter 2:21-24 (AMP) *"For even to this were you called [it is inseparable from your vocation]. For Christ also suffered for you, leaving you [His personal] example, so that you should follow in His footsteps. (22) He was guilty of no sin, neither was deceit (guile) ever found on his lips. [Isaiah. 53:9] (23) When He was reviled and insulted, He did not revile or offer insult in return; [when] He was abused and suffered, He made not threats [of vengeance]; but he trusted [Himself and everything] to Him who judges fairly. (24) He personally bore our sins in His [own] body on the tree [as on an altar and offered Himself on it], that we might die (cease to exist) to sin and live to righteousness. By His wounds you have been healed."*

23.) It does not matter if the abuser was ever caught, got away or if the abuser was left unknown, he/she will be judged for their actions toward you. By whom?

So that you can live how?

And by His wounds (that occurred during the abuse or sin that you experienced, and you must now give over to Christ completely) you are ______________?

24.) Jesus is familiar with grief, sorrow, shame, being despised, abuse, insult, suffering, and yet He still trusted God. If you have difficulty in trusting, can you learn to trust in Him now that you are aware of the level of relationship He wants to have with you? Explain your answer.

Homosexuality.

The assumption that a boy who was molested by a man will grow up to be homosexual or a child molester is neither true nor fair. The same goes for a woman. If a man molests a girl, we assume the reason she later appears masculine and becomes a lesbian is because she hates men. But, more inconspicuous feelings come when a warm feeling comes over a victim when they are touched, like hugging, by a member of the same sex. Ambivalent emotions are sending out fireworks of confusion and fear. We are created to respond to emotional touch, physical touch, and sexual touch. The warm fuzzy you may have felt during a hug probably was innocent on your part. Perhaps you have scolded yourself for having normal feelings for so long that until now you misinterpret your emotions, and convince yourself that you are being perverted, thereby shaming and showing contempt for yourself.

Can a person have a very close and loving relationship with a member of the same sex but not be homosexual or bi-sexual? Of course they can. Love that is from God is pure and untarnished. It is people who make the good seem dirty. Let's look at King David and Saul's son, Jonathan, in the early years of their adulthood.

1 Samuel 18:1-4 AMP *"(1) When David had finished speaking to Saul, the soul of Jonathan was knit with the soul of David, and Jonathan loved him as his own life. (2) Saul took David that day and would not let him return to his father's house. (3) Then Jonathan made a covenant with David, because he loved him as his own life. (4) And Jonathan stripped himself of the robe that was on him and gave it to David, and his armor, even his sword, his bow, and his girdle."*

Comment: David went to the palace with Saul after he had killed Goliath and after the prophet Samuel had anointed David to be the next king. Jonathan, who by worldly expectations was heir to his father's throne, gave David his robe and battle equipment. He was acknowledging that David would be king, and a great friendship was formed at that moment.

1 Samuel 20:17 (AMP) *"And Jonathan caused David to swear again by his love for him, for Jonathan loved him as he loved his own life."*

Comment: Without understanding the background of verse 17, there could be an assumption of a relationship between the two men that is beyond friendship. But there is nothing more than a bonding that goes deeper than brothers.

Then the unthinkable happens. David ran from Saul for many years, hiding in caves and living in tents, avoiding killing the king or being killed by him at all cost. David has such great respect for God's anointing on the King of Israel, that he will not kill him even to protect himself. By now he had made a covenant, or a promise, to Jonathan that he would never kill him or any member of his family, when David does take over the throne. The killing of heirs to the throne was customary when a new king took over as a measure to prevent future war.

But in the midst of battle, Saul killed himself; and Jonathan and two other sons of Saul who were fighting at his father's side are also killed. The man who killed them, thinking David would be very pleased, came to him and gave the news. Remembering his promise of safety to Jonathan, David goes into a deep grief and has the man killed also. Then David wrote a lament, or grief song, to be taught to all of Israel so that they would never forget Jonathan. The second to last line in the song, if taken literally, can be misinterpreted.

2 Samuel 1:26 (AMP) *"I am distressed for you, my brother Jonathan; very pleasant have you been to me. Your love to me was wonderful, passing the love of women."*

Comment: But we must remember, other cultures have different customs, and open expressions of physical and emotional love are accepted and expected, even in same gender relationships. True

                                    Caught in the Act of Grace Women's Bible Study

friendship is not affected by the unexpected changes in our lives; we should learn what the ancients wrote on the subject of true love. Hebrew "Friendship is an entire sameness, and one soul. A friend is another self." Phileo love is the kind of love that consists of the glow of the heart. It is the response of the human (soul) to what appeals to it as pleasurable. Phileo is the word used to speak of friendly affection.

Colossians 2:2 AMP *"[For my concern is] that their heirs may be braced (comforted, cheered, and encouraged) as they are knit together in love, that they may come to have all the abounding wealth and blessings of assured conviction of understanding, and that they may become progressively more intimately acquainted with and may know more definitely and accurately and thoroughly that mystic secret of God, [which is] Christ (the Anointed One)."*

Comment: Note Paul, in the New Testament, and how he was treated in Acts by both the women and the men. Acts 20:37 (AMP) *"And they all wept freely and threw their arms around Paul's neck and kissed him fervently and repeatedly. Men and women alike hugged, held each other and kissed each other. Touching is a normal and needed part of the human experience."*

Forgiving does not necessarily bring restoration of a relationship. It is likely that the relationship with the perpetrator will not be restored. If the perpetrator was a member of your family then your relationship with your family may not be immediately restored. Sometimes relatives need to get to a point of letting go of their own bitterness. You are not responsible for anyone's emotions but your own. Forgiving is an act of the will and impacts one's relationship with God. The act of forgiving is not optional as relayed by Jesus in His sample prayer, which we refer to as the Lord's Prayer:

Matthew 6:12, 14-15 (NKJV) *"12) Forgive us our debts, as we also have forgiven our debtors. 13) For if you forgive men when they sin against you, your heavenly Father will also forgive you. 14) But if you do not forgive men their trespasses, your Father will not forgive your trespasses."*

25.) Write down 10 good things about yourself. Do not give in to the temptation to skip this question completely or to not do all 10.

1.

2.

3.

4.

5.

6.

7.

8.

9.

10.

Prayer:

Dear God:

In Jesus' Name, Amen.

REMINDER: Remember to Journal daily…

Chapter 7

Betrayal

Who I Am In Christ

Read daily. Put your name in the blank.

The Word of God Says...

________________ is reconciled to God...2 Corinthians 5:18

________________ is a citizen of the Kingdom of God...Ephesians 2:19

________________ is the righteousness of God...2 Corinthians 5:21

________________ is a partaker of His divine nature...2 Peter 1:4

________________ is called of God...2 Timothy 1:9

________________ is God's workmanship...Ephesians 2:10

________________ is an ambassador for Christ...2 Corinthians. 5:20

________________ is the Bride of Christ...Jeremiah. 3:14-15; John 3:27-29

________________ is Jesus' "little lamb"...John 21:15-17

________________ is a partaker of Christ...Hebrews 3:14

Objective:

- Explore the person you really are.
- How to regain trust.
- The importance of breaking sexual soul ties.
- Spiritually cleanse yourselves through a system of steps.

Inspiration:

> *2 Corinthians 4:1-2 (NKJV)   "Therefore, since we have this ministry, as we have received mercy, we do not lose heart. (2) But we have renounced the hidden things of shame, not walking in craftiness nor handling the word of God deceitfully, but by manifestation of the truth commending ourselves to every man's conscience in the sight of God."*

The Journey Continues…

Shame and Guilt

The utter and resounding fear of exposure is that someone you love has found out a secret about you. Perhaps it is something that you have hidden for a long period of time. Perhaps God is saying to you, "no more secrets", as He did to me. Now is the time for change and it begins on the inside – from the depths of your private world.

The tyranny of a secret is that you must always remember what it is in order to keep it. You must also remember who knows the secret so you don't accidentally let it slip out to someone else. Even in the subconscious, there are reactions to memories that surface at the most distasteful moments.

When a secret is exposed, trust is desperately hoped for but not counted on by someone who has been deeply wounded in the past. If we want to start and keep the momentum of obedience to God, then it is important to remember that He is the only One who will never betray us. When opening up about a secret it can feel as if you are hanging on a limb high in the air and being asked to let go, or standing on the mountain of hiding the past and being told that the only route to freedom is to jump off the edge of the cliff of every secret, into the unknown, to have Hope catch you. This kind of Hope, will never betray, wound, or use your past as a weapon to cut you deeply in the heart or stab you in the back. God will never give anyone an assignment that the Holy Spirit is not completely and wholly prepared to help you to completion.

My past kept me fearful that people would find out ALL the truth about me, and then hate me. I would tell myself "Preachers wives do not have a past like that". My dependence on others to determine my value or self-worth, and hoping to be myself with no more pretense in their presence, was a very high price for their approval.

The cost of exposure and betrayal is trust. Trust lost is hard to win back by a betrayer, but even harder to be given back by the one betrayed. In some abusive relationships trust should never be given back. But for others, this is exactly what God asks us to do. Proper and well-defined boundaries are a safety and comfort zone. Out and out refusal to forgive is the hurt that keeps on hurting. Walls without gates not only keep people out, but they also keep you locked in a virtual prison of your own doing.

When the time came for me to expose my past publicly, there were several things I had to walk through. The first was that I had to have a measure of healing for myself. I could not give away what I did not have. Over the next two years, God used several ministries and a post abortion Bible study to do just that for me. I had to face the wound I had allowed that went against my very instinct to nurture - the betrayal of my own motherhood in 1983. This decision was at the cost of my oldest son Joshua's life. At the end of that study I told God, "You give me a mountain and I'll shout from it!"

The second part was where the climbing of the mountain began in my quest to claim victory over it. Like Much Afraid in the book "Hinds Feet on High Places" by Hannah Hurnard, there were many valleys, craggy places, and steep slopes. For me that translated into times I bled and became frustrated. My great comfort through it all was I was never alone; God was always just a call away. I had begun the transforming journey of change in every aspect of my personhood - mentally, physically, and spiritually.

The hardest of all the changes was the third area – me. The person I used to be was the Darla that everyone was familiar with, and who they really liked. The old me was the one that was needy, and kept her relationships pretentious and therefore superficial. In my friendships, I needed some people to be my spiritual guides – thus they had importance. I needed others to be my mentors. If I kept them happy, no matter the cost to my family or myself, then they continued to like me. If I was physically available to them, then I was always included in their plans even if I did not want to do what they liked to do. But to change myself meant that they had to meet an entirely new person. My concern was that the "new Darla" might be a person whose personality might clash with those of my friends. The "new me" was not the "old me" that they liked, so many of my friendships became entrenched in turmoil. But to let go of the past I had to continue to move toward the person God had created me to be, the hidden person of the heart who was crying out to be revealed.

The graciousness of how to accept me as I changed was not always there on my part or the part of others. Some friendships slipped away quietly, lovingly, expressing how proud of me they were. Others made the bumpy journey with me. But it seemed the ones I thought I knew best, and the ones I trusted, behaved the worst. These friends of mine were the keepers of my secrets, and when I exposed them to others, it not only took away the devil's power over me (fear), but their power over me (telling on me). No longer did I have to take extra care to keep those people content in my relationship with them, lest they tell on me. There was no longer a "stake" of potential betrayal held over me in my subconscious. Not one of them would have maliciously told anyone my past .... until I did.

My greatest test in founding this ministry happened when I first started it. In Job Chapter One, he gave sacrifices unto the Lord, in the event that his children would sin and die. Then his greatest fear happened anyway and they did die, but not in sin. My greatest fear came to pass also. Exposure of the secrets of my past caused people to turn away from me. They did not like me anymore.

Embarrassment caused by "their preacher's wife" telling the secrets from her past, in church, and the ensuing publicity following having her picture on the front cover of the local newspaper, caused quite a stir in our small town. Then to have my story, and the healing that God gave me, spread not only all over the state but throughout the nation through magazine articles and newsletters was an even greater insult to some people.

These people would ask me, "Why are you doing this?", and "Don't you know you are hurting your husband and children?" My reply was, "Because God told me to and my family supports me in this." The elders of my church even held a surprise meeting with my husband after church one night, locking my children outside the building but not out of earshot. Them screaming at him to "stop your wife" seeped through the walls of the building and into the ears of my preteen babies. Listening to men that my children respected tell my husband what kind of person they felt I had become, shot pain into their hearts and the bleeding of tears flowed out of their eyes. Looking into their faces when they all came home, followed by months of continued scenarios like this one, made me want to stop with all my heart, soul and body. I would have quit if not for two elements: God and two of the elders began to check on me daily to make sure I knew how sorry they were for wounding me personally even though they did not care for this type of ministry!

At the same time I looked into the eyes of women who were walking behind me as I plowed through this tangled maze of healing. My tears, caused by the betrayal of people we considered friends, were always followed by tears of joy at the healing freedom of long-tortured souls in the women who came to the Bible Studies. These women and God made me continue to breathe in and out - one day at a time and walk forward in spite of the betrayal that came at the cost of not just me, but my entire family.

Our trust in God through it all made us stronger and helped us to forgive every one of those people over time. Each betrayer, in his or her own way, did ask for forgiveness. No healing came overnight. It took years for some to be willing to move past the embarrassment of their own actions.

The cost of betrayal can be high, especially during the innocence of youth when expectation of trust is there. Then like a wisp of steam dancing out of a teakettle just beginning to boil - it is gone. But for the old or the young, does it need to stay gone forever? Perhaps not. You see, steam rises into the air and evaporates. Next, it condenses, falling back to earth in the form of precious rain. The rain sinks into the earth to replenish our water supply, and once again, we have life giving water with which to fill the teakettle. In simple terms, water may leave, but it also returns. A molecule of water will never return the same as it left, but will return in a changed manner, and will still able to refresh and nurture. Trust may be lost to betrayal, but it can return, changed but refreshing.

1.) What was the very first betrayal you can remember? (Does not necessarily have to be sexual abuse.)

2.) Did you ever put your trust back in the person(s) involved in that betrayal? If yes, did they betray you again? Explain.

There are many people in the Bible and today who were betrayed and betrayers. The very people whom God cherishes betray Him through the breaking of His commandments, the killing of His prophets, widespread immorality, unstable families, and the list can go on.

3.) Although God is full of grace, the trust He puts in His people is shattered many times. Have you ever completely put your trust in someone, only to have it shattered by their actions or attitude? What could you have done differently in that situation to keep yourself from being hurt?

Read Hosea 1:1-3

Why would God tell His prophet to marry a prostitute? He had decided to use Hosea as an example to Israel of what they had done in their relationship with Him. They had prostituted themselves to other gods and rebellion. What He had given to them, they had given to Baal. Hosea trusted God and followed His instructions to the letter, even though from a worldly view he appeared to be going against God.

4.) Do you have times when you question whether you hear or have heard from God in the midst of obeying Him? Give an example of one of those times of doubt.

Read Hosea 3:1-3

Gomer (Gomer is a female), after bearing Hosea two sons and one daughter, walked out on Hosea. The life he led was very different from what she was accustomed to. As many people today do, she went back to what she knew even though it was wrong - prostitution. She left behind what was good, the love of a good and Godly man and her children.

5.) What are some of the old habits you had in your life? Double check the ones you still do and be honest.

______smoking ______drinking ______drugs ______eating disorders ______lying

______cheating______stealing______laziness______workaholic______promiscuity ______other (explain)

                    Caught in the Act of Grace Women's Bible Study

6.) In what ways is it easier to be the way you have always been, rather than change and become different?

7.) Name three habits or character traits you want to change in your life?

    1.

    2.

    3.

Of those three, tell how each could be associated with your former sexual abuse. If they are not associated with your abuse, then tell where you feel they came from.

What can you do, to change each of these?

8.) If God created you and has a plan for you according to Jeremiah 29:11, do you believe He has a "you" that is His perfect creation?

What do you think you would be like? Describe the "you" that God created physically, emotionally, mentally and spiritually. Take your time and ask God to help you. Use your journal if you need more paper.

Gomer, whom Hosea had never had to purchase as his wife, now purchased her back in Hosea 3:2. The purchase price for her was the price of a slave. Gomer had gone back to the life she knew and had taken it a step further by allowing herself to be enslaved to that life.

9.) Have you ever made the declaration, "I will never ___________ again!" only to find yourself doing that exact same thing, only this time it is worse? What was one of those times?

10.) Did you need help to get out of that situation, but could not ask due to early trust and betrayal issues?

Hosea was a man of God and did not go to get his wife back from her pimp until God told him to. He stayed home and took care of their children, worked, prayed, and probably cried out of a broken heart for the woman that he loved. She had left him for not one man, but many. He had given all that he had to her including his name, and she had betrayed him. Yet, when God told him to go after her, he did not hesitate. Once he had found his wife and purchased her back as his slave, he took her back home. Legally, he could have had her stoned or divorced her, but God wanted her back.

Regaining Trust.

Read Hosea 3:3-5

Hosea had to have a change in his wife if they were going to live out their lives together. She needed discipline in her own life. He could not make her learn through discipline, but he was willing to be an example to her.

11.) What did Hosea tell Gomer she was going to do?

12.) What did Hosea tell Gomer he was going to do?

13.) After many days, what did God tell them that they would do? "*5) Afterward shall the children of Israel return, and seek the LORD their God, and David their king; and shall fear the LORD and his goodness in the latter days.*"

14.) What do you think Gomer did that betrayed Hosea the most?

15.) What did Gomer do to regain Hosea's trust?

16.) What would your abuser or people in general, have to do to regain your trust?

Part of processing of a trust issue or any other issues that are wounding is the desire to make the guilty party pay for their actions. Holding someone accountable for their actions is a good aspect of processing to a good end. Making someone pay penance for their actions until you feel like they have paid a proper penalty for their actions, where you are the judge and jury, is wrong processing.

What is paying penance? It is making someone sorrowful for sins or faults that you feel they should pay for. If you make yourself the decision maker for what a person has to do to make amends with you, then you are setting yourself up as their judge. The Bible says that only God is to judge.

Read Matthew 7:1- 6.

17.) Are you requiring more than you have a right to require according to the example that you have been given? What is the beam that you have in your eye?

18.) Do you believe that God "understands" the requirements you place on people in order to earn your trust?

19.) What part of your requirements do you think God would ask you to stop doing in order for Him to restore to you the innocence of your childlike trust in others?

Read Matthew 7:7

There is always common sense that must bring balance to every situation. God is a common sense God and He gives us all a measure of common sense. Long ago I realized that if I had something, a thought, a scripture verse, something physically available to me; not all would be as excited about "it" as I was. For me to share my precious possession or thought with someone who may not understand or be excited for me was as though I was casting my pearls before swine. Pigs are intelligent but they are also very nasty creatures in nature. They will eat their own if given the opportunity.

20.) Are you concerned that someone has ill-feelings toward you often? Are you suspicious of people? Do you live in a world that is full of foggy realities, distorted truths, or are you unable to be objective in your life? Choose any one or more of the above and elaborate on them. Use your journal if you need more space to write.

21.) If these reactions did not generate from your sexual abuse, where do you think these attitudes come from?

22.) What can you change in your life to make these reactions stop?

> ***If you have never had sex outside of your abuse or a marriage relationship, please skip this section and move on to Spiritual Recovery.***

Sexual Soul Ties.

In the act of sex, whether forced or consensual, the two do become one not only in body but in spirit. Many times, we try to remove the spiritual side of healing from sexual abuse because of discomfort or misunderstanding of the Bible.

If you were asked to believe that God answers prayers, it would be easy for you to do so, because prayer is commonly accepted and desired. If you were asked if the first person you desired to have sex with, be it a boyfriend or husband, was still a part of you in the form of memories, your answer would be "yes". Even if the experience was disappointing, he would still be referred to as, my first, in the form of the possessive word "my".

If the first person or following people you consented to have sex with are a part of you, and the memories of the ones you did not approve of or are ashamed of, are still there and are a part of you, then why would we try to convince ourselves that the abuse is not connected to us?

Steps to Breaking Sexual Bonds.

By Sydna Masse

Our classes are filled with individuals who were not abstinent before marriage. Yet rarely do individuals work to rid themselves of the weight of these past sexual memories. Some are freed of these bonds when they originally come to the Lord. Others need an exercise to help them understand the depth of the sin they experienced and the incredible redeeming love of God. Second Corinthians 4:2 (NIV) states:

"... we have renounced secret and shameful ways; we do not use deception, nor do we distort the word of God. On the contrary, by setting forth the truth plainly we commend ourselves to every man's conscience in the sight of God."

"In understanding spiritual warfare, we know that the truth is an essential element in our defense against Satan." as outlined in Ephesians 6:10-12 (NIV):

"Finally, be strong in the Lord and in his mighty power. Put on the full armor of God so that you can take your stand against the devil's schemes. For our struggle is not against flesh and blood, but against the rulers, against the authorities, against the powers of this dark world and against the spiritual forces of evil in the heavenly realms."

"Remember that one of the parts of God's armor was the "sword of truth" (Eph. 6:14). Later in Revelations 12:10, it is written that "they overcame him (satan) by the blood of the Lamb and the word of their testimonies. Since sexual immorality is a sin against the body, helping (participants) confess this can be a strong step towards salvation and healing efforts."

No Contact

One important concept to embrace in working through these memories in (the sexual abuse) class is to steer them away from re-establishing a relationship with a past lover. We have seen marriages dissolve when such contacts are made during the healing process. Many husbands are intimidated by their wives attending a class where they are working to (recover from a memory of a past relationship or abuse). The current relationship may be at a difficult point and the memories of the love of the other person could be all that's needed to allow Satan to destroy the marriage. Writing letters they never send could be a useful way to overcome this yearning to contact.

There are a few exceptions to this rule. When my initial testimony was aired on Focus on the Family broadcast, 10 million people tuned in. It was important that I contacted "Alan" to inform him that our secret would be outlined. While I never shared his name publicly, and still do not, he needed to be prepared. Later I would locate their names on the Focus database and send my own confession and apology. My husband read and approved my letter to "Alan" before it was sent. While he never responded, I felt compelled to correspond. The only way a person can contact a previous lover is with the specific permission of their spouse.

Grieving their Lost Innocence

Many times our (participants) were not completely responsible for losing their virginity. These women have been victims. These initial sexual experiences can spiral them toward a promiscuous lifestyle. Love equals sex. Yet many report that they don't enjoy any of these sexual encounters. What is amazing is that they continue to participate in casual sex and can't see how this hurts them.

(For the Post Abortive only) In the pregnancy care counseling rooms, these women are often scared of the prospects of parenting because of the poor examples they had for parents. When they abort, they experience another form of sexual abuse in the actual procedure. Their private areas are touched sometimes harshly and their maternal bond that tells them to "protect their child at all costs" is severed. So much happens to them during the abortion that it's easy to see why so many are mentally unstable afterwards.

When they get to the point of acknowledging their part in the abortion decision and begin to grieve, many times they are mourning multiple experiences. As long as they are not using this grieving to somehow eliminate the responsibility for their own sin, this mourning can be a helpful part of healing.

Removing Tangible Reminders

I remember my husband coming up from the basement one day holding my old photo album. He asked, "Can I get rid of these pictures of your old boyfriends?" From the look on his face, I knew I had to agree but part of my heart wanted to keep these tangible memories. Tom was right and he took great delight in destroying these pictures.

It's amazing how many people keep these old souvenirs from past relationships. Maybe it is a special necklace, earrings or even pressed flowers. The spoken word through old letters can be very powerful. Normally the least we maintain is photographs. How many mementos do you have in your possession? Understand that these items can be triggers to memories of sexual immorality that can affect their/your walk with the Lord. Pray about destroying these reminders as part of the breaking soul ties exercise.

Sharing at Home

Here is something to consider: if a person was sexually abused by a family member, their confession has other implications. I spoke to a woman who was repeatedly raped by an older cousin. Even to

  Caught in the Act of Grace Women's Bible Study

this day, 20 years later, she has rarely shared this secret with anyone and must interact with this person during family events (i.e., reunions, weddings, funerals, etc.). She is concerned that should she share this truth with her husband, he will want to use force against this person. Unfortunately her husband has achieved a friendship with this person and is curious as to why his wife doesn't share the same level of respect. While she has shared that sexual abuse was part of her past, relaying the person's identity is still something she is unable to accomplish. In her desire to protect her family from division, and a possible physical fight, she remains silent about this secret.

Sharing outside of class is an issue each person must pray about. While the timing might not be right, they may be able to share in the future. Simply offering them a safe place to share with friends is a very healthy first step. Should the spouses be supportive of this process, the women can really find themselves falling in love again at an entirely new level.

The Two Shall Become One

The thought of sexual encounters, whether heterosexual, homosexual, oral, emotional, sight (pornography), etc., connecting one to another as a spiritual union never crosses anyone's mind when the act of sex has begun. Instinct and lust seem to have a way of shutting down the mind. But consider the following verses.

1 Corinthians 6:15-20 (AMP) *"Do you not see and know that your bodies are members (bodily parts) of Christ (the Messiah)? Am I therefore to take the parts of Christ and make [them] parts of a prostitute? Never! Never! (16) Or do you not know and realize that when a man joins himself to a prostitute, he becomes one body with her? The two, it is written, shall become one flesh. [Gen. 2:24.] (17) But the person who is united to the Lord becomes one spirit with Him. (18) Shun immorality and all sexual looseness [flee from impurity in thought, word, or deed]. Any other sin which a man commits is one outside the body, but he who commits sexual immorality sins against his own body. (19) Do you not know that your body is the temple (the very sanctuary) of the Holy Spirit Who lives within you, Whom you have received [as a Gift] from God? You are not your own, (20) You were bought with a price [purchased with a preciousness and paid for, made His own]. So then, honor God and bring glory to Him in your body."*

The only union that is seen as good and blessed by God is one between a husband and a wife for the purpose of making them one flesh and having children. When my husband and I married, there was one thing that I asked of God on my wedding day. Giving my husband my virginity was not an option in the natural. Long ago it had been lost and for that I was deeply sorry. Not only did I feel like Gomer marrying Hosea as my husband is a minister, but my only chance at a blood covenant with him would soon be lost forever if God did not answer my prayer. As I sat in my room and prayed, I asked God for several things. First, prepare me for the new life He was about to send me in to. Second, restore my virginity. Not for my sake, but for my husband and the gift that should have been his and his alone. I wanted to give my new husband all of me. That night, God gave me what I asked for. Although it was a small amount, there was a blood covenant between my husband and myself on our wedding night. Why do I share such an intimate detail of my private life? Because if I can give one person the hope of restoration then I am willing to give the testimony of God's grace and mercy to me. My virginity meant a great deal to me once I understood the importance of the marriage covenant and the preciousness of lifelong bond to one person.

In society, it is considered macho for a man to lose his virginity before marriage. For a woman the expectation is for her to be willing to "put out." You must understand that the value and worth that you place on your own body is evident in how you treat it. Giving up the only gift of yourself to someone who does not have enough respect for you to live the rest of their lives committed to you will result in a lot of pain.

EXERCISE: Use a page in your journal and begin to list every person in your life with whom you have had a sexual encounter. Remember that oral sex is still sex, therefore those people also should be listed. If you cannot list the person by name then use a description. It is important that you consider each person as individually as possible. This may take a few days to accomplish and please do not post these names in your Bible Study book. Bring them to class with you with the understanding that at no time are you to give these names to anyone. This exercise is between you and God, no one else. During the next class there will be time set aside to let you individually turn over each of these ties to God, releasing you from the bond of joining yourself to another out of wedlock.

Spiritual Recovery

Sexual abuse is the most intimate form of betrayal. This is due to God's Word to the man and woman in Genesis 1:22-25. What God created as a lifelong bond was soon perverted by Satan.

After sexual abuse has occurred, we begin to look at ourselves in a different way. We begin to feel different about ourselves. Negative feelings begin to surface and take root in our thinking. What does it take to remove those feelings? Acceptance that someone has violated you, but in accordance with the Bible, Satan has turned what God called good into something perverted. This leaves you with a decision. I can recover physically and look normal and healthy. I can recover mentally over time and for the most part, function in a normal way. I can recover emotionally as long as no one expects something out of me that I cannot give. However, spiritually, I cannot look into the face of God and not feel changed, dirty, unlovable or worthy. Why is this? The spiritually perverted part of the perversion came into you and became a part of you at the moment of becoming one.

Hosea separated from his wife for a time to not only allow her time to learn self-discipline, but to also allow spiritual cleansing to take place in her. He did not want all the baggage she had picked up from every one of her sex partners. Was this time of cleansing full of incantations, repetitive prayers, souped-up spiritualism, or "repeat after me so you can be clean" type prayers? No. God asks us only to be simple and sincere.

What are the steps of spiritual cleanliness?

1. **Acknowledge** your sin. The abuse was not your sin, but bad behavior you chose afterwards is your sin. Do not use your past as an excuse for poor behavior or as crutch to continue in bad choices.

2. **Confess your sin.** Tell a trusted person and allow them to be a healing aspect of your life. Do not blurt out your sins to someone you know just because you have known them a long time. They may not be able to help you. Trust after betrayal can put a damper on this, so do not allow your past to stop you now. Remember, the abuse was not your sin, bad behavior afterward and up until now is your sin. Name each one of your sins exactly.

3. **Ask God for forgiveness**. Trust Him that if you ask in a simple and sincere way, He hears you, loves you, believes in you and forgives you.

4. **Believe** that God has forgiven you and claim your forgiveness. Do not let doubts creep back into your mind and begin to convince yourself that this is stupid. Trust and believe. Do not waiver. Now that you have forgiveness, do not let it go. Do not let people or slip-ups make you feel like you have to start over with the forgiveness process. God does not expect you to be perfect. He only expects you not to turn away from Him. People can be cruel. Ignore them!

5. **Remain forgiven**. Now is the time to lock into church and begin to grow. If you have been in church your whole life and are not active, you are not growing. If you have never been to church and are scared of church people, find a church where you know people and where the Bible is taught. If you are a mature Christian and have just now come to grips with this one part of your life, now is the time to appreciate Jesus' dying on the cross all the more, and reach out to help your fellow sisters who are still lost and dying inside - victims of their own wounds.

Prayer:

Dear Lord:

In Jesus' Name, Amen.

REMINDER: Please remember to Journal daily…

Chapter 8

Owning Anger

Who I Am In Christ

Read daily. Put your name in the blank.

The Word of God Says...

______________is Created in the image of God...Psalm 119:73

______________is Promised "rest"...Exodus 33:14; Hebrews 4:9

______________ is "Chosen" by Christ...John 15: 16; Ephesians 1:4

______________is Protected by God...Deuteronomy 7:6-8; Joshua 1:3-9

______________is Forgiven...Hebrews 9:14; Colossians 1:14; I John 2:12

______________is Blessed...Psalm 1:1-3; Ephesians 1:3

______________is Able to sleep without fear...Psalm 3:5; 4:8

______________is the "Apple" of God's eye...Psalm 17:8

______________is Strong in the Lord...Psalm 18:1-2; Ephesians 6:10

______________is a Child of God...John 1:12-13; Romans 8:14-15

Objective:

- Know what Post Traumatic Stress Disorder is and how it can affect your life.
- Know the difference between outward aggression and passive aggression.
- Understand the need to forgive.
- Begin the steps of letting go of anger and rage that may be inside.

Inspiration:

Leviticus 25:43 (AMP)

"You shall not rule over him with harshness (severity, oppression), but you shall [reverently] fear your God." [Ephesian. 6:9; Colossians. 4:1.]

Psalm 4:4 (AMP)

"Be angry [or stand in awe] and sin not; commune with your own hearts upon your beds and be silent (sorry for the things you say in your hearts). Selah [pause, and calmly think of that]!" [Ephesians 4:26.]

Ephesians 4:27 (AMP)

"Leave no [such] room or foothold for the devil [give no opportunity to him]."

The Journey Continues...

Stress can overwhelm

Looking in the mirror one morning I noticed something about myself, the tendons on the sides of my neck seemed to be in a constant strain. Several weeks later as I reviewed a taping for our church I noticed the same thing. My entire adult life I knew that there were times when I felt certain emotions that made me feel very uncomfortable. In a grand effort to control those emotions it now appeared that my body had finally betrayed me. It had begun to show the signs of strain. Privately my family and I knew that I had developed numerous stress-related problems; migraines, TMJ, and dysfunction. My neck had become stiff and no longer could my head turn from side to side, the right side of my face stayed numb the majority of the time, and loss of appetite was always a concern. The strain of "self-control" had taken its toll. Something had to change.

The problem was that I was painfully aware that I had a temper and in a heartbeat it would show. Even if I did not yell or throw a fit, the sharp and harsh tones of my voice mixed with the cutting look on my face told everyone around that it was time to step away from this little stick of dynamite. No matter how hard I tried to stop looking or sounding mean, my face and actions would betray me over and over again. The feelings of frustration would only increase as I tried to appear what the Bible calls self-controlled, mild, meek, kind. The more I tried to be mild and meek, the more I wanted to slap somebody. Now how is a minister or Christian supposed to get by with that? This also added to my stress!

Then there was the crying. If the urge to cry ever came it felt like a tsunami was sucking the life out of me only to overwhelm me with a flood of tears and raw emotion that would carry me away into untold places. Gut wrenching sobs would come up out of the depth of my soul and what felt like loud and embarrassing wailing would take over my being. This simply would not do. How could I let go and behave in a way that I felt I may not return from? Refusal to cry in public when those emotions came dangerously close to the surface only added to the internal stress I was experiencing.

Even the simple things of life became frustrating over time. Cooking a meal only to have no one come to eat it, picking up the clutter around the house that no one would help pick up, and putting the dirty dishes in an empty dishwasher because my family did the "drive by drop" into the sink. And the killer for me - coming home from a long day at work to a dirty kitchen and demands for a meal while everyone is watching TV day after day. My husband would say to me, "where there is no ox there is no litter. Do you want no ox or no litter." Some days I wanted no litter and to have ox for dinner! Most days, life was tolerable.

Internalizing anger will take its toll on you and expressing it improperly will take its toll on your relationships. In the end, the very thing that you desire to change in yourself must be addressed and new coping strategies must be put into place in order to be who God created you to be. Perhaps I will never be the mild, meek little woman that is full of mercy. Perhaps you will never be like the person that you admire the most. But rest assured that God did create each of us individually for a purpose. You are uniquely made and wonderfully loved by a creator who has plans for you. Just as your fingerprints are yours and yours alone, you are God's fingerprint on the world. He did not make you the way you are to change you, but to temper you with fire until the imperfections are burned out of you and you are completely His to use, however He chooses if you allow Him to.

Post-Traumatic Stress Disorder

Post-Traumatic Stress Disorder (PTSD) is an anxiety disorder brought on when a traumatic event is experienced that includes intense horror, helplessness or fear. Not everyone will develop PTSD, but the likelihood of experiencing it at some point in life is significant when sexual abuse trauma is experienced. In the United States, seven to eight percent of people will develop PTSD, with combat veterans or sexual assault victims ranging from ten to thirty percent; women are twice as likely to develop PTSD as men. Although references to PTSD have been made for as long as human beings have existed, it was brought into public knowledge by the Viet Nam Veterans after returning home from war.

The same anxiety that you may experience from time to time is the same anxiety that others also experience. The assumption that there is something "wrong" with you is in fact true but it is also something that can be controlled or cured. Not everyone who experiences PTSD has long term effects from it. The longer the trauma was experienced, especially as a child, the more likely the effects will be long term. In this case, the seeking out of professional help may be an option that you have not considered before, but should now. The shame in needing professional help is not in the fact that you go, but in the pride of refusing to go. If you or a family member had a heart condition or was diabetic, you would seek out a professional immediately and do all that they require to give you a healthy life. The same goes for mental health needs. We should never assume that mental health is secondary to physical health. Many times it is mental strain causing physical problems that we experience but are unwilling to address. Address the source of the stress and the TMJ, migraines, dysfunction or heart attack will go away.

A friend of mine once became so irritated by a man that she had a heart attack at work and had to be taken to the hospital in an ambulance. The man had come into her office regularly to discuss and challenge her on an issue that was not ever going to be solved. They simply had two differing opinions on their religious beliefs. Instead of asking the man to stop this discussion she tried to be kind, allowing him to overstep what she could tolerate. Everyone knew that she was being irritated, including the man who was doing it. One day she had enough and her internal stress load overcame her desire to be kind and she had a heart attack. After that day, the man apologized for his pushiness and never brought up the topic again. She was embarrassed that she allowed it to go to that level and discovered that tolerance does not include being pushed to mental overload.

Although some may disagree, the need for overall health in the spirit, body, mind and heart should not only include trusting in God for our healing but using every avenue that He has made available to us. Using food, drugs, alcohol, work, or even religion as a means of avoiding the health issues that you have need of addressing is wrong. Therefore, it is encouraged by this Bible study writer, if more help is needed or if this study is a means of opening a door for help for you, please seek out professional help and don't stop until you get it.

Post-Traumatic Stress Disorder Symptoms[2]

Symptoms for PTSD will typically appear within three months of the event, but in some instances they may not occur for many years. These symptoms may include:

- ✓ Flashbacks and or distressing dreams associated with the event.

- ✓ Anniversary reaction—distress at certain times of the year associated with the event.

- ✓ Efforts to avoid activities, thoughts or feelings associated with the event.

- ✓ Feelings of detachment or estrangement from others and an inability to have loving feelings.

- ✓ Diminished interest or participation in activities that once were an important source of satisfaction.

- ✓ Hopelessness about the future.

- ✓ Hypersensitive, hypervigilant, panic attacks.

- ✓ Depression.

Symptoms of PTSD in sexual abuse trauma

In comparing PTSD to symptoms of PTSD in sexual abuse victims, you will be able to see that the symptoms are the same or very close to the same. There is not a "childhood sexual abuse syndrome" that we can look to, or an "adult sexual abuse syndrome" either. The evidence only concludes that a trauma has occurred but not the type of trauma.

Children:

- ✓ Agitated behavior, dreams that frighten them, expressing the abuse in play or activities such as art
- ✓ Age inappropriate displays of seductiveness or sexual behavior. (This does not include infant exploration of body parts. This is natural discovery. The key word is inappropriate display, such as Ken and Barbie being placed in sexual positions, or talking about the opposite gender in adult terms.)
- ✓ "acting out," such as cruelty or running away
- ✓ "acting in," such as withdrawal or depression
- ✓ Self-inflicted injury or suicide attempts
- ✓ Regressive bed wetting, incontinence, chronic constipation, or inability to hold bowel

Adults:

- ✓ Relationship, intimacy or sexual issues – promiscuity or dysfunction
- ✓ Low self-esteem or isolation – feeling of being flawed or bad
- ✓ Shame and guilt – overreacts in telling or hiding
- ✓ Inability to trust others or themselves
- ✓ Discomfort with being touched
- ✓ Re-victimization – abusive relationships and causing themselves to be wounded repeatedly
- ✓ Fear of feelings – a need to control feelings and behaviors (own or others)
- ✓ Flashbacks
- ✓ Insomnia and other sleep disorders
- ✓ Amnesia – memory loss, forgetting pieces of childhood
- ✓ Depression – including suicidal thoughts and attempts
- ✓ Anxiety – hypervigilant, panic attacks, fears and phobias, fear of violence
- ✓ Drug and alcohol abuses
- ✓ Eating disorders
- ✓ Social and economic failures – overachiever, underachiever, feelings of being an imposter, fear of being "found out who they really are on the inside"
- ✓ The more grotesque the abuse is the more prominent the PTSD symptoms in the short term, but the more common affects occur over long term and carry the weight of the causality

Types of Anger

Outward Aggression

Outward aggression is the most obvious type of aggression. It is hard not to see or hear someone who is outwardly aggressive. There are many ways to express outward aggression other than physically or verbally. Emotional and mental abuses can be used by both an outward and passive aggressive person. The use of pointing out flaws or criticizing is also a way of outwardly expressing anger.

1.) Are you outwardly aggressive? List the things that you do that are signs of your aggression to others or yourself.

2.) In conversations, do you point out others flaws, point out your own flaws, or tell what someone has done to you? Write out a recent example of this.

Read Ephesians 4:29-32 (AMP)

"29) Let no foul or polluting language, nor evil word nor unwholesome or worthless talk [ever] come out of your mouth, but only such [speech] as is good and beneficial to the spiritual progress of others, as is fitting to the need and the occasion, that it may be a blessing and give grace (God's favor) to those who hear it. 30) And do not grieve the Holy Spirit of God [do not offend or vex or sadden Him], by Whom you were sealed (marked, branded as God's own, secured) for the day of redemption (of final deliverance through Christ from evil and the consequences of sin). 31) Let all bitterness and indignation and wrath (passion, rage, bad temper) and resentment (anger, animosity) and quarreling (brawling, clamor, contention) and slander (evil-speaking, abusive or blasphemous language) be banished from you, with all malice (spite, ill will, or baseness of any kind). 32) And become useful and helpful and kind to one another, tenderhearted (compassionate, understanding, loving-hearted), forgiving one another [readily and freely], as God in Christ forgave you."

3.) Fill in the blanks using the above scriptures.

Let no_________________________________, nor ___________________ nor ___________________ or ___________________ [ever] come out of your mouth, but only such [speech] as is good and ____ of others, as is fitting to the need and the occasion, that it may be a ____ (God's favor) to those who hear it.

And ____[do not offend or vex or sadden Him], by Whom you were sealed (marked, branded as God's own, secured) for the day of redemption (of final deliverance through Christ from evil and the consequences of sin).

Let all _______________ and _______________ and ___________ (passion, rage, bad temper) and _______________ (anger, animosity) and _______________ (brawling, clamor, contention) and _______________ (evil-speaking, abusive or blasphemous language) be banished from you, with _______________ (spite, ill will, or baseness of any kind).

And become_______________________________________, tenderhearted (compassionate, understanding, loving-hearted), _______________ [readily and freely], _______________ .

4.) Do you recognize any description of yourself in the scriptures listed above? If so, what are they?

When speaking to or about someone with aggression, there is always going to be someone around who is listening. We all have a great desire to be liked by people or at least certain people. But in an effort to get grace, we sometimes forget to give grace. The gift of grace should be given in our actions and our speech. Verse 29 says, "but only such [speech] as is good and beneficial to the spiritual progress of others, as is fitting to the need and the occasion, that it may be a blessing and give grace (God's favor) to those who hear it."

5.) Do you give the gift of grace in your speaking to and about people so that others who are around or the person that you are speaking to, whether listening or overhearing your conversation, make spiritual progression or are blessed by your words?

6.) If your answer was no or sometimes, please list things that you say and a better way of saying it.

Things I say: Better way of saying it:

Passive Aggression

Some of the angriest people I have ever been around have been passive aggressive. What makes a relationship with this type of person difficult is that they always feel justified in their actions because they did not say anything wrong that could be perceived as hurtful, or they say just enough to wound but not destroy the other person. The constant picking at a scab will cause a scar and the passive aggressive habits are that of scab picking. They never make you bleed nor do they let you heal.

To a passive aggressive person, to say anything that comes across as slander or even anger is to not be "holy" or nice. Aggression is judging in the eyes of the religious people of the Bible and the religious people of today. But does that make silence any better than words? No it does not. Silence is usually louder than words and is often used as a weapon to cut to the soul of people it is aimed at. "I did not say anything!" is a lame excuse to the wounded recipient of a passive aggressor. Holding grudges, making people pay penance for their actions until you feel like they have paid long enough to finally be forgiven, avoidance of phone calls, deleting of emails. These are not acts of forgiveness but instead are judgmental acts.

In a discussion with one woman she described her mother in this way. "She does what our family now calls 'sea gulling'. She swoops in, dumps on your head, and then flies away quickly. Then we are all left looking at each trying to figure out if some action should be taken with what she just said." This mother has found a way to express her thoughts in an inappropriate way that actually wounds her family. Therefore, she is continually wounded because none of her family wants to be around her.

Other excuses for passive aggression are "I have been so busy", "you are always so busy," "I knew that you would not have time……," "I just forgot," "I had a headache," on and on it can go.

7.) When was the last time you got so mad that you yelled or behaved in an outward expression of anger?

8.) Are you the kind of person that will not speak to someone for hours or days? If so, explain the benefits of not speaking to someone?

9.) How does avoidance help to resolve the issue or does it prolong the issue?

10.) Do you believe that you have control over your emotions when you don't express your feelings or hold grudges, or do your emotions control you in these situations?

11.) What can you do to change the way you react to situations that anger you?

12.) What is the difference between holding a grudge and avoiding someone because they hurt you in some way?

What does the Bible say about Anger?

13.) Read each of the following verses and write what it says about God's wrath.

Nahum 1:2-6

Romans 1:18

Psalm 103:8-10

14.) Read each of the following verses and write what it says about Jesus' anger.

Mark 3:5

John 2:13-16 (What made Jesus angry?)

Hebrews 4:14-15 (Does Jesus understand our anger?)

15.) Read each of the following verses and write what it says about our anger.

Ephesians 2:3

Ephesians 4:26

Matthew 7:1-5

Our Declarations

The first time we realize that we are free from the control of someone who once controlled us we may have said or thought consciously or subconsciously – "I will never be controlled again," or some other declaration. The Bible says in Deuteronomy 30:19 *"I call heaven and earth to witness this day against you that I have set before you life and death, the blessings and the curses; therefore choose life, which you and your descendants may live"*. In light of this verse, there is an opportunity to do one thing or the other; bless people or curse people, bless ourselves or curse ourselves.

In order to not be controlled a person has a free will that must be dealt with. What does that mean? It means that you get to choose how you treat others just as they get to choose how they treat you. The struggle between good and evil inside of people is always there, therefore to not be controlled someone will often times become controlling.

Many year ago, and before I became a Christian, I made a declaration that I felt gave me great power. I had been abused for many years and at 16 years old I had an abortion that I did not want to have. In the aftermath of the abortion I became so angry that I made two declarations. The first, no one will ever control me again. The second was even more dangerous, Hell hath no fury like a woman scorned. When I said it, I meant it. For the next few years I found myself looking for ways to wound men no matter how mean or manipulating I had to get. Certain men that I felt had betrayed me; I searched for them in order to hurt them by whatever means necessary. Typically, I went for their hearts in an effort to break their hearts as mine had been broken. Unfortunately several who did not deserve to be wounded were wounded. In my anger I felt justified as I intentionally walked away from men who had grown to love me. More than a few times I refused to allow my conscious to overtake my need for revenge as grown men cried when I walked away. Not that I was especially worthy of love, only I had learned how to get into a man's heart and hurt him greatly. How? Men taught me. The vicious cycle was set in motion for me and still is in many today.

Several more declaration examples: I'm out of here………; If I don't acknowledge you, then you don't exist…………; How can I ever trust myself, I never saw it coming………..; I don't have to take this……..; I just can't talk to you………; I would rather be anywhere but with you……….

16.) Have you made a verbal or heart declaration about your life? If so, write it or them out.

Psalm 4:4 (AMP) *"Be angry [or stand in awe] and sin not; commune with your own hearts upon your beds and be silent (sorry for the things you say in your hearts). Selah [pause, and calmly think of that]!* [Ephesians 4:26]

17.) Use the space below to repent and ask God to forgive you of your past declarations.

Dear God,

In Jesus' Name, Amen

Anger versus Rage

18.) Write out the definitions of the following words:

Anger –

Rage –

Have you ever considered that you may be angry about your past abuse? Perhaps you feel as though you have dealt with all anger and have forgiven the people who have hurt you. Do you feel anxiety when you think of spending time with certain people? If you answer yes to either of these questions, consider the following story.

Several years ago I began thinking about my relationships with others and wondering why I struggled with people. Friendships always seemed to struggle, family relationships were in crisis too often, my relationship with my husband and children was becoming increasingly difficult. The love that I wanted to experience between myself and God seemed to have a barrier of some kind. I knew God's word. I had studied and taught it for many years. I tried with all my heart to live it but there was always a missing link. Prayer and time at the altar never seemed to break the barrier down. Begging God daily to change me and help me to love with all of me only could get me so far. The idea of teaching a sexual abuse Bible study weighed heavily upon me, but because I could not find one that I felt comfortable with the excuse to not do anything was sweet relief.

Then one day during a worship service at a church God spoke clearly to my heart. He said, "I want you to go to Russia." Crying, I said, "Okay; I will go where you send me." The thought of going to Russia was a little overwhelming, but I knew that if God wanted me to go, He had a reason, and I would be safe.

Three years later a friend called and asked me a question out of the blue. "I am putting a missionary team together to go to Russia. Do you want to come? Oh, and I want you to teach on Sexual Abuse. You will be the only member of the team to do that part." My first response was "Yes, I will go, God

                    Caught in the Act of Grace Women's Bible Study

told me to go and my husband agreed." I had six months to prepare to teach on a subject that I knew I was called to teach but had avoided with all of my heart.

Two months before we left I was still desperately praying and asking God what I was supposed to teach. I called another friend who is a prayer warrior and asked her if she could carve out some time to meet with me once a week for a while and pray with me. I knew something inside of me was stuck but I didn't know what or why. I felt that I had forgiven everyone that I could and life was as wonderful as anyone should expect with my past. As we began our weekly prayer sessions together she brought several books for me to read on my own. One of the books held my attention. It was "Total Forgiveness" by R.T. Kendall. I found what I needed, what forgiveness really was, not what I had been taught it was. That is what I decided to teach in Russia.

Armed with my book and Bible, plus another book on sexual abuse recovery, we headed out on this adventure. Never in my life had I considered that I would go to Russia to discover my past still had a hold on me in a way that I never could have imagined.

Once there, our group settled into our rooms at a small hotel in Perm. Then our leader began briefing everyone on how our conference would run and how the recovery classes that we would conduct would be laid out. I was to assist in the recovery classes before the conference, then teach my two workshops. Along with this briefing, we were to all be instructed in recovery exercises that we could illustrate to the women. At a previous conference, a lady that I had befriended told me, "I have an exercise that you need to see. I want to do this exercise with you." She was also on this trip with us and the exercise was one that we would be using. I volunteered.

We had decided to use my sexual abuse past for the exercise with one specific abuser that I knew I still had a problem with down deep in my heart. No matter how hard I tried to forgive him, it was only words and not from my heart.

There were nine women present, all were watching and praying, and there was an intercessor that stood behind me and prayed for me the entire time. What happened shocked me. As she asked me to talk to my abuser as though he were there and to tell him that I forgave him, a rage came up from inside of me. It was so complete that I could not imagine feeling the cold steely hatred that I had inside of me. I was consumed. She never gave up on me, pressing forward she encouraged me to see him as a human being who had problems. I had only been able to see him as an old man who had become a monster, hatched from an egg, and never a child or young man who was loving or kind. She tried from every angle to make me see that I needed to let go of the rage and forgive him with all of me, but I stubbornly hung on.

I had gone to him many years earlier expecting an apology, only to be turned down and told that he had never done anything bad to me. He said that what he had done was not wrong but loving. The anger that I felt when he had died and took my apology with him had settled into my soul. But now I was staring into the face of my soul and it was not a pretty sight.

After almost an hour of talking me through the exercise I began to break. I could not connect with him as a person or even a human, but there was someone that I could connect with, my daughter. She is the remake of me but in a good and right way. All of the hopes and dreams that I have had in my life, she has accomplished. Strong discouragement from me of following in my footsteps has never made her sway from the path that she is walking. The difference between us is that she is not wounded by a past that is like mine, she is merciful, kind, forgiving, and easy to get along with. Often I have wondered if she is who I was supposed to be had I not been abused. I connected with her. I was able to forgive my abuser because I knew that she would have forgiven him, no matter what. She is my hero in so many ways, and as I said that day, "My daughter would forgive him no matter what, so therefore I want to be like her and I choose to forgive him too."

The anticipation of forgiveness that I thought would make me feel better at this point was not there. In its place was the feeling of eternal torture, or Hell. As I sat there a surge of torment shot through my body and I began to scream in a guttural way. The words came to my mind as clearly as though they were said out loud, "Do not come where I am!" I call this my Lazarus Moment. I got the mental vision of Lazarus sitting in the arms of Abraham, and the rich man in Hell asking for Lazarus to give him a drink of water to cool his tongue. In this moment I realized that I had received a drop of what it felt like to be in Hell for eternity. That un-forgiveness, bitterness, resentment can all take me down the same path. Any pain that I have felt on this earth, in my entire lifetime, was no more than a drop of what it would be like if I was in Hell for eternity.

The desire to forgive and let go of the past must be realized in a way that does help you to reconnect with the person who has wounded you, even if it is only a small amount and for a moment in time. Grave clothes came off of me that day. I was able to finally take the chains off that kept me connected to him, through realizing that on earth the abuser never cared to make things right, but in eternity he was sorry for what he had done. His reward has been given, but mine is still in my hands. I choose to be forgiving like my daughter is forgiving, with all of my heart. What I had felt was not anger it was pure rage, then it was gone.

Read Luke 16: 19-31

19.) Have you ever considered the level of anger that you feel toward certain people? On a scale of 1-10 with 10 being the highest, how anxious would you feel if you confronted the person who abused you face to face?

20.) If a physical reaction is present that is strong like anxiety, there is a good chance that there are unresolved issues that need to be addressed. Write out every name of every person that makes you feel anxious.

Owning Your Anger

Anger is a demand. You must value me, you must trust me, you must love me, and you must respect me. When we are not given what we want we can very easily turn the problem toward the other person in the form of a demand. We say that if you do not give me what I want I will make you sorry, by being mean to you or being angry with you.

That's the real thrust of anger. A demand that also demands others meet your demands. Even though you seldom put the demands into words, they are there inside the feelings, energizing the resentment. "What if I said what I feel, if I really made my demands clear? Then I could stick to them, or cancel them, laugh at them and forget them..."

Freedom from being dominated by anger begins by tracking down the demands made on others. We begin by recognizing them, and admitting them out loud speeds up the process of owning the anger.

Then one has a choice:

> (1) Negotiate the demands that matter, or

> (2) Cancel the ones that don't.

Freedom comes as one willingly and openly is candid in facing the demands made on others. Even silent, passive anger places demands that is binding in relationships.

The fact is no one can make you mad; you choose to get mad. Whoever angers you, rules you.

Write a separate letter to each person whose name you wrote down. Be sure that you say to them all that you feel needs to be said. If you think of more people write as many letters as you wish. Bring them to the next class with the assurance that no one will read your letter or letters.

In your journal, write something about each person that brings you comfort about them, even if it is through someone else, like my daughter. Then express your forgiveness of that person in your writing. You may be doing this exercise out of obedience instead of feelings but forgiveness starts with obedience not feelings.

If you feel like you have no one that you are at odds with or need to forgive, perhaps you have mistreated someone or have never asked to be forgiven. This exercise may be necessary for you to do from the aspect of being forgiven instead of giving forgiveness.

Anyone who says all is good and has nothing to forgive, or to be forgiven of, would make me question the realness of their relationships with people. Either you are so closed with people that you cannot have a relationship with people that shows your good and bad points, or you wound people with no regard for your actions. One thing is for sure, hurting people hurt people and even the best attitude or heart is not perfect.

Allow the Holy Spirit to show you the doors of your heart that are closed and then allow Him to open them…one at a time.

Prayer

Dear God:

In Jesus' Name, Amen

REMINDER: Remember to Journal daily…

1. Reference: MedicineNet.com, Posttraumatic Stress Disorder (PTSD), Medical Author: Roxanne Dryden-Edwards, MD, Medical Editor: Melissa Conrad Stöppler, MD
2. Reference: Child Sexual Abuse, National Center for PTSD Fact Sheet
3. Reference: Julia Whealin, Ph.D., Child Sexual Abuse, National Center for PTSD Fact Sheet
4. Reference: Caring Enough To Confront: How To Understand & Express Your Deepest Feelings Toward Others, By David Ausburger

Chapter 9

What Are Boundaries?

Who I Am In Christ

Read daily. Put your name in the blank.

The Word of God Says...

_________________ is washed clean from my sins...Isaiah 1:18

_________________ is always in God's thoughts...Psalm 139:17-18

_________________ is loved by God...Jeremiah 31:3; Romans 8:37-39

_________________ is the salt of the earth...Matthew 5:13-14

_________________ is valued by God...Matthew 10:29-31

_________________ is at peace with God...Romans 5:1

_________________ is dead to sin...Romans 6:1-18

_________________ is the temple of the Holy Spirit...1 Corinthians. 6:19-20

_________________ is a new creature in Christ...2 Corinthians. 5:17

_________________ is crucified with Christ...Galatians 2:20

Objective:

- Know the definition of a boundary and its use.
- Know what is expected of a Christian when we forgive.
- Understand what burdens we carry when we do not let go of the past.
- Be better in control of your relationship decisions.
- Learn how to develop relationships that are by choice and are respectfully put into place and firmly managed.
- Know your value and being in control of your life, NOT controlling.

Inspiration:

Isaiah 42:1-4 (NIV) *1) "Behold! My Servant whom I uphold, My Elect One in whom My soul delights! I have put My Spirit upon Him; He will bring forth justice to the Gentiles. 2) He will not cry out, nor raise His voice, Nor cause His voice to be heard in the street. 3) A bruised reed He will not break, And smoking flax He will not quench; He will bring forth justice for truth. 4) He will not fail nor be discouraged, Till He has established justice in the earth; And the coastlands shall wait for His law."*

The Journey Continues…

Many times in early years of my life I have stood on a porch at night staring up at the stars, tears streaming down my face, and asked God, "Why _____________? Why did You create me? Why am I this way? Why does no one love me? Why did he leave me? Why did my friend betray my trust? Why do I feel so lonely? There have been times that I have actually asked people why I feel so incredibly lonely."

How does anyone stand in the middle of a room full of people and feel so utterly and completely alone. I have noticed the lonelier I feel, the more my mouth runs, the more my mouth runs, the more I say things that I regret such as hurtful comments or demanding statements that I don't mean. The more hurtful my words become, the more quiet I get and the more people do not want to talk to me. The final results are my loneliness increasing all the more because I've proven to myself that no one wants to be my friend. Except people who should not be my friend.

Also, in many relationships I have been in over the years there has been a pull – tug experience, like the game of Tug of War that we played as children. Whoever is the strongest wins the game, whoever is strongest, controls the relationship, the weaker loses. Only from time to time is a relationship on an equal status level. Although hard to imagine to the sexually abused, there are people who love them just the way they are and have no hidden agendas. They like being around them "just because" and are willing to give and take in the relationship. The abuse victim was told at the time of the abuse, in verbal or non-verbal communication, "you have no choice in where I (the abuser) fit in your life. I will do with you whatever I please". In response to this, the boundaries that were previously known or taught became dulled and confused, or perhaps were erased all together.

No longer do some of the sexually abused understand when someone of a stronger personality is present, they do have the choice to tell them they are no longer welcome to be in relationship with them. When stronger personalities are controlling her/him, the child inside of her/him, that was so scared and hurt, reacts in a grown up way. Extreme reactions can occur to seemingly small actions. Over the top emotions flood out of her/him when she/he knows circumstances do not warrant the way she/he feels. Out of control becomes the norm and fighting back when pressure is applied is always a welcomed or unwelcomed option.

The other option is to be used and pushed, expecting to not have value to anyone and accept any kind of attention given. These are the women, and sometimes men, who are in danger of allowing abusive relationships to continue in their lives because they don't know they have choices. They believe that they deserve to be punished for their past. The boundaries in relationships are once again null and void. Being of equal value and importance to other people seems to be something that will never be a part of life. They do not dream of being in control of life or defining who they are, based on their relationship with Christ, who says that they is of extreme value and loved.

1.) What is your "idea" of boundaries in your life?

2.) Look up the definition of boundary and write it. Was your "idea" of a boundary correct?

The Difference Between Forgiving Others and Personal Boundaries

Once you know what a boundary actually is, you can now discover how to interact with others in the healthy way.

3.) Read the following verses from the Amplified Bible and briefly explain what they mean to you.

Romans 12:1 *"I APPEAL to you therefore, brethren, and beg of you in view of [all] the mercies of God, to make a decisive dedication of your bodies [presenting all your members and faculties] as a living sacrifice, holy (devoted, consecrated) and well pleasing to God, which is your reasonable (rational, intelligent) service and spiritual worship."*

a) Explain:

Romans 12:2 *"Do not be conformed to this world (this age), [fashioned after and adapted to its external, superficial customs], but be transformed (changed) by the [entire] renewal of your mind [by its new ideals and its new attitude], so that you may prove [for yourselves] what is the good and acceptable and perfect will of God, even the thing which is good and acceptable and perfect [in His sight for you]."*

b) Explain:

Romans. 12:3 *"For by the grace (unmerited favor of God) given to me I warn everyone among you not to estimate and think of himself more highly than he ought [not to have an exaggerated opinion of his own importance], but to rate his ability with sober judgment, each according to the degree of faith apportioned by God to him."*

c) Explain:

Romans 12:4 *"For as in one physical body we have many parts (organs, members) and all of these parts do not have the same function or use"*

d) Explain:

Romans 12:5-6 *"5) So we, numerous as we are, are one body in Christ (the Messiah) and individually we are parts one of another [mutually dependent on one another].6) Having gifts (faculties, talents, qualities) that differ according to the grace given us, let us use them: [He whose gift is] prophecy, [let him prophesy] according to the proportion of his faith"*

The body we're talking about is Christ's body of chosen people. Each of us finds our meaning and function as a part of His body. But as a chopped-off finger or cut-off toe we wouldn't amount to much, would we? So, since we find ourselves fashioned into all these excellently formed and marvelously functioning parts in Christ's body, let's just go ahead and be what we were made to be, without envious or prideful comparison of ourselves with each other, or trying to be something we aren't. If you preach, just preach God's Message, nothing else;

e) Explain:

Romans 12:7-8   *"7) [He whose gift is] practical service, let him give himself to serving; he who teaches, to his teaching; 8) He who exhorts (encourages), to his exhortation; he who contributes, let him do it in simplicity and liberality; he who gives aid and superintends, with zeal and singleness of mind; he who does acts of mercy, with genuine cheerfulness and joyful eagerness."*

f) Explain:

Romans 12:9 *"[Let your] love be sincere (a real thing); hate what is evil [loathe all ungodliness, turn in horror from wickedness], but hold fast to that which is good."*

g) Explain:

Romans 12:10-15 *"10) Love one another with brotherly affection [as members of one family], giving precedence and showing honor to one another. 11) Never lag in zeal and in earnest endeavor; be aglow and burning with the Spirit, serving the Lord. 12) Rejoice and exult in hope; be steadfast and patient in suffering and tribulation; be constant in prayer. 13) Contribute to the needs of God's people [sharing in the necessities of the saints]; pursue the practice of hospitality. 14) Bless those who persecute you [who are cruel in their attitude toward you]; bless and do not curse them. 15) Rejoice with those who rejoice [sharing others' joy], and weep with those who weep [sharing others' grief]."*

h) Explain:

Romans 12:16-19   *"16) Live in harmony with one another; do not be haughty (snobbish, high-minded, exclusive), but readily adjust yourself to [people, things] and give yourselves to humble tasks. Never overestimate yourself or be wise in your own conceits. 17) Repay no one evil for evil, but take thought for what is honest and proper and noble [aiming to be above reproach] in the sight of everyone. 18) If possible, as far as it depends on you, live at peace with everyone. 19) Beloved, never avenge yourselves, but leave the way open for [God's] wrath; for it is written, Vengeance is Mine, I will repay (requite), says the Lord."*

i) Explain:

Romans 12:20-21 *"20) But if your enemy is hungry, feed him; if he is thirsty, give him drink; for by so doing you will heap burning coals upon his head. 21) Do not let yourself be overcome by evil, but overcome (master) evil with good."*

j) Explain:

4.) Think of someone who has hurt you with words or actions recently, or from your past, and write each action from the verses in Romans that you are currently doing to help restore your relationship with them. Check off the phrases from the above verses that you have done for the person you have thought of.

______ refusing to strike back with insults or gossip.

______ telling others only of the good in them.

______ trying to get along with them.

______ not dreaming of revenge.

______ let God do the judging because He CAN take care of it.

______ inviting them to dinner or taking them food if they need it.

______ generously loaning them whatever they need.

______ not letting evil get the best of you but get the best of evil by doing good to them.

Romans 12 overall message is to:

- know who you are as a Christian,
- know that God created you and gave you certain gifts,
- use your gifts to be a benefit to the body of Christ and others,
- look for the good in everyone including your enemy,
- bless your enemy then and therefore kicking the devil in the teeth because he wasn't successful in making you bitter or in taking your own revenge.

5.) Did God say anywhere in these scriptures that you are required to be in a close relationship with someone you consider an enemy or someone you don't feel you can trust?

The Bible does not say you are required, as a Christian, to be in relationship with an enemy. Perhaps you have been taught in order to show forgiveness, you MUST be in relationship with an enemy. Now you are in a dilemma. Your first instinct is one of self protection, then a desire to please, followed by the questioning of your own ability to decide what your relationships should look like with others. Most people will do one of two things; walk away from the relationship and those who are imposing pressure, or give in and be in a relationship with someone who has not earned the trust that is necessary to be in a relationship with them. God says in Matthew 5:44 to love your enemies and pray for those who persecute you. I have found that I love well and pray often for people that I may never see again, but who also have the desire to wound me greatly if I continue to allow them to be my friend.

6.) Was there even one scripture verse that said to do all of these things, and then invite him to your house to hang out? NO. Nowhere in the Bible are we taught that to care for the needs of an enemy or simply care for an enemy means that you have to spend your time with them. Does generosity mean that you must be trapped in a relationship with someone who causes you harm?

Be in Control Not Controlling.

What happens when our own personal moral code has been violated such as when someone insists that their way is the only way. For the sexual abuse survivor, this has already happened. Perhaps you were young when the abuse occurred and you were not sure of what a moral code was much less what how to live by it. As we grow older and look back on the things that have been done to us, we realize two things, it was wrong and it never should have happened. For the adult survivor of childhood abuse, it is the child who was wounded and the adult who remembers. Therefore memories are distorted because of time and reasoning. For the adult survivor of adult sexual abuse, a serious lack of control in your own life had taken place. The realization that someone else had control of your life or death for a period of time is mind numbing. In both instances, boundaries that should have never been crossed were.

So who is in control of the boundaries that protect us today if no one but the abuser had control of our protective boundaries back then? Exactly when should we fight back and when should be play dead? When do we behave agreeably and when do we tell that we are being wounded? These are two questions that I remember thinking in the midst of assaults on several occasions. What is necessary for my survival at this moment?

As a child I remember the butterflies in my stomach at the thought of getting a spanking from my parents or my grandmother if they found out what was happening to me. Never did it cross my mind that if the abuse was brought to light I would be protected, only that I would be in trouble. After all, that is what my abusers told me would happen. "You would be a tattle tale and get in trouble. Nobody likes a tattle tale and a bad girl. Besides, you don't want to get me in trouble too do you! No one would really believe you over me anyway."

The most intimate act that a person can have in their lives is the act of sex. Even though it is abuse, sexual abuse is still the act of sex. Therefore, when someone forces another to perform an act of intimacy against their will, or even out of obligation, there is a sense of no control. No control means that someone else has control over you in the most intimate way known to you, leaving you with a duty to yourself to never allow that to happen again under any circumstances.

Later, the emotional scars that wrap our minds in memories as sharp as fragmented glass, reinforce the duty of self-protection. Do you choose to fight back or play dead to survive the day-to-day relationships that you are in today? Do you understand that the reactions that your emotions take in relationships today are the same emotions that are filled with the fragmented glass of abuse? The cutting and bleeding that you did then is the same cutting and bleeding that you do today, either to yourself or those who try to get close to you.

Self-protection can be a brutal task master. This occurs when the person you trusted taught you that no one else will protect you. Self-protection through passive or outward aggression will always leave you alone and lonely. Keep others at arm's length; hoping that they will come no closer is more than anyone can bear.

Matthew 11:30 (AMP) *"For My yoke is wholesome (useful, good--not harsh, hard, sharp, or pressing, but comfortable, gracious, and pleasant), and My burden is light and easy to be borne."*

7.) What does Matthew 11:30 say carrying God's burden is? What does it say that His burden it not?

8.) Draw a picture of what your **Abuse Burden** looks like to you in the space provided. Use words if needed, but show what it feels like to you to carry around the pain of your past and perhaps your present.

9.) Check off the following statements that you have made in your lifetime:

______ You tell what someone else has done to you more than two times.

______ You repeatedly ask the question "Why do things keep happening?"

______ You expect people to do what they say and then are angry when they don't do it.

______ You refuse to ask for help because you know that you will be turned down.

______ You make a joke out of things that hurt your feelings to cover over the wound, but later have a pity party of some kind.

______ You are always looking for the answer to your problem. There is always something wrong with you physically or mentally.

______ You have not spoken to someone who used to be special to you for a very long time and you will not be the one who makes the first move.

______ You ask the question, "Why do I always have to make the first move? I didn't do anything wrong."

The Eternal Victim

Sitting down with my husband for a cup of coffee and conversation one day, the conversation turned personal. This time it took a road that I was not interested in, the one that led to my door.

For several months we had been tag teaming, going to see a counselor, about some things in our marriage that we had come to a standoff over. I believed that I was right, and he believed that he was right. It was causing problems in our relationship. Never one to sweep something under the rug, I had finally convinced my husband to go to the counselor with me the first time, then he was willing to go alone after that. To my delight, he was really benefitting from these counseling appointments and our lives were beginning to change over time.

Then the fatal morning came when he felt he was ready to share what he was working on in our marriage. Until now we had been doing our own assignments from the counselor, and not sharing. Then he dropped the bomb on me. He explained that he had learned that all sexual abuse victims take on an ETERNAL VICTIM mentality and, from their point of view, everything happens to them. Ha! The conversation was now over and the coffee pot contents were poured down the drain. He said that I had an eternal victim mentality; I decided to prove him wrong. The only problem was, every time I became upset after that conversation I found myself blaming someone else for the upset.

It was always someone else that started the problem, someone else who made the issue, someone else who was supposed to get something done and didn't, someone else.......

    Caught in the Act of Grace Women's Bible Study

Ugh! He was right; I was continually setting myself up to be a victim!

How do I get over this one? The thought of it made me pretty angry. Then I began listening to the people that I counseled with or led in groups and realized, they were are all in the same boat. Not one of them made it through the sessions without an eternal victim mentality on some level or in their past. Some were so caught up in their eternal victim mentality that they could not function in life on a normal level. They were always fighting to make things happen or mad at someone for not letting something happen. They seemed to get what they deserved or were going to give what someone deserved. "Poor, poor me", and "Why does this keep happening?" are mottos embedded into the banner of their lives. The funny thing is that the more they deny that they act this way the worse they usually are. Even now as you are reading you are probably thinking "what a bunch of losers" not realizing that you are talking about yourself!

An eternal victim is a person that believes that everything happens TO them. They carry their pain like a badge of honor, readily telling their experiences, their aches and pains, or standing back quietly and suspiciously waiting for the next person to wound them. This is a burden that has to be remembered, played over and over in their minds, so they can remember why they are supposed to be miserable.

"Another definition not as commonly used is one that says a person thinks the future only holds bad things for them. If you do not get the promotion it is because Mr. Johnson was out to get you. Not because he found you playing on the Internet every day. Your best friend called and said she could not have dinner with you. She is always doing that to you; not showing. You'll show her. You won't invite her when you go out again! Instead, remember that she has just started school and you did call her at the last minute."[1]

If you checked off any of the questions on number nine, you could be an eternal victim.

What about Rejection?

Do you concern yourself with fear of rejection? Are you devastated for months at a time if you feel rejected by someone? Years ago, shortly after the birth of my son, I invited a friend to go shopping with me. We were going to the mall in the next town, just the girls, no children, husbands or time restraints. I was so excited about spending time with another woman just doing girl things. It had been a long time since I was able to do something like that because of our schedule and two small children at home with no relatives to help out. My husband knew how excited I was and agreed to keep the children for the day. When the time for her to pick me up came and went I decided to give her house a call to see if something may have happened. After all I had money burning a hole in my purse and permission to spend it from my husband. After several rings, her husband picked up the phone. Cheerily I asked him if she had left yet, to which he made several stuttering noises. Then he said, "Hang on, let me get her." Seconds ticked by then he was back on the phone apologizing. She had asked him to call me earlier that morning to let me know that her mother had called and she had decided to go shopping with her and her sister at the mall instead. She was now mad at him for not calling me, refusing to get on the phone to tell me herself. I really do not know what my reply was, but I believe it was something like "that is okay, I understand" just as I hung up the phone.

This woman had just devastated and devaluated me all in one act of rejection. I sat on the bed and cried for hours. My husband did his best to console me, even offering to go shopping with me. This couple was friends of his from his younger years and I had only come into the picture in the last few years, therefore he felt responsible for their selfish and thoughtless behavior. In the end, I never asked her to go anywhere again. Our friendship was damaged and trust was broken. Behaving as though she had done nothing wrong was the way we lived for the rest of the time we lived in the same town. But neither have I forgotten the hurt of being left behind when I was so excited to go.

What would be a better way to react to the situation. First, realize that the self-centeredness she displayed would spill into any relationship that she was involved in, not just ours. Not expecting too much from her as a friend would have been a benefit. Second, realize that she was not rejecting me as a person. She simply did not think about her rudeness. Knowing I was a new mom, trapped in a home with no time to make friends never crossed her mind. Living a life that revolved around themselves is how some people live, with never a consideration of the people they wound along the way. Third, I should have taken my husband up on his offer and spent the day with him and my children. They have disappointed me from time to time over the years, but never with intent to wound.

You may be thinking of a situation from your past that warrants justifying your anger. Your sexual abuse may be your wound that won't heal. Perhaps you were treated unkindly by a "friend" just as I was. Whatever your reason for refusing to be friendly today, it is time to get over it.

"People who lack social confidence and who constantly fear getting judged and rejected by others may have been born with a very sensitive nervous system. But it's also probable that they grew up in a family that didn't offer them very much love or reassurance. They may even have been neglected or abused.

When you grow up feeling very insecure, you constantly fear that any friendship or relationship around you can vanish at any second. Because of the faulty thinking patterns you have grown up with, you are always convinced that any seeming rejection must all be your fault. You fear being rejected because you are not good enough. You fear approaching other people socially because any rejection by others triggers a nightmare of cruel self talk inside you."

Do you make friends easily or do you hold back in a crowd of people, watching them first to get to know them before you allow yourself to greet them?[2]

Do you expect your friends or family to say no when you ask them to help you, or do you refuse to ask because you are convinced they will say no? (Some people actually do say no regularly. They are not who I am referring to.)

Do you expect friendships to fail after a certain length of time?

Are you afraid of expecting the best for your life?

What can you do to change any of the questions that you have answered yes to?

Protection with a Gate

A boundary is a wall unless there is a gate. Boundaries are intended to keep people at the distance you decide they should be from you in your life. If you never allow people to come close to you, you have a wall and have barricaded yourself into a life of loneliness, even in a crowded room. You can only have friends if you show yourself friendly.

Gates are openings in a fence or wall intended to allow people into your life and to let them leave your life. Boundaries with gates are healthy, but they are not to be locked if pain can be seen coming either. Sometimes the greatest gift you can give is the gift of good-bye to someone who needs to be separated from you.

Like the tide ebbs and flows, people will come and they will go. But you will only be satisfied if you allow yourself to experience each relationship without expectation or fear. It is your decision where people fit into your life, close to you or at a distance. You can choose to answer the phone or let it ring.

God will bring you the right people to be your friend in a Godly way if you ask. So many of us grab for the first friendly face, or we befriend someone who makes us feel good at the moment. Friendships and relationships that are built over time are not "instant oatmeal" fulfilling, but are deep and meaningful. Trust should never be handed to just anyone, it must be earned. This takes time and evidence. We teach our children not to get into cars with strangers and yet we give out personal information on internet chat rooms, My Space, and Facebook on a regular basis. We tell others to

Caught in the Act of Grace Women's Bible Study

stand their ground with a friend, family member or boss when asked to do something we know is wrong and yet we allow others to use us regularly.

If you are someone who jumps in and out of relationships or find yourself jumping into the same kind of relationship over and over, perhaps a good look at why you allow those people into your life would be very informative. Then a good hard look at yourself may reveal to you who you really are. Sometimes when God introduces us to ourselves, we don't like who we meet.

Whether you are a push-over or aggressive, submissive or dominating, quiet or loud, fearful or fearless, you can change who you have become with hard work and determination. Boundaries are walls with gates. They are healthy and should be established in every person's life. It is your decision who is allowed inside your boundary and who is kept outside of it.

Whether it is your relationship to God or to others, if you take away the freedom to choose, you take away the ability to love. It is only when you are free to choose and disagree that you are free to love. When you live without freedom you live in fear and love dies. You cannot actually love someone if you don't feel you have a choice to love or not to love.

13.) In your relationship with God, do you feel freedom

- To love Him: _______________
- To not love Him:_____________
- To obey or disobey Him: __________

God will protect your right to make choices no matter which one you choose. He will protect your right to go to heaven and He will protect your right to go to hell. Without choices, there is no serving Him because you love Him. Serving God out of fear or mandatory obligation because your mother or father told you to is not what He wants. He wants us to serve Him and allow Him into our lives because He created us and loves us. If we have no freedom to be ourselves with God, we will have no freedom to be ourselves in our human relationships.

14.) What are some new boundaries you can set with people now that you know forgiveness does not require relationship?

16.) Do you find yourself accepting whatever way people decide to treat you?

17.) Does this acceptance make you feel:

______angry   ______subdued   ______controlled   ______unsure of yourself _____explosive   _____vengeful   _____resentful   _____good

18.)   When your boundaries are set, are you willing to follow through with reinforcing them, no matter how it makes you feel? Explain what you may try doing differently with someone, i.e.: If you feel unsure of yourself in a crowd, try speaking to people in a friendly manner.

Your value as a person is in no way dependent on how others expect you to treat them. It is based solely on what God thinks about you. It depends on you!

Below is an example of how to make good choices. Even if you have never been in this position, read the following example and write what you believe the best choice is according to the person you are becoming not the person you used to be. Kindness should prevail if you are a strong boundary setter and firmness should prevail if you allow people to manipulate you.

Example: Your father molested you and you have spent your whole life pretending that nothing is wrong. Finally at the age of 30 you can't hold your emotions in check anymore. You go through a Bible study to help you reconcile your feelings. You learned that you don't have to allow him to control the relationship by making you feel like you have to treat him as though he never abused you. In fact, although you confronted him and he denied it, you are no longer comfortable being at family gatherings. You treat him with respect and honor, because he is still your father. You feel it is okay to meet all of the requirements of being a daughter, Christmas presents, birthday cards, etc. But, you want to set a boundary of no phone calls, no emails, no weekends at his house, no coming to your house, and your children are not allowed to be around him.

19.) Choose one or as many of the following that you would do. Be honest with yourself.

_______ Your sister calls and she wants to meet you at Dad's house for the weekend, but when you say no and offer for her to come to your house, she becomes angry and accuses you of being unforgiving. You give in and go to his house to please your sister.

_______ The whole family decides to come to your house for Christmas, then calls you to let you know. They say that they didn't include you in on the decision because they knew you would say no. They want you to get over your past and move on, so just cooperate this time, and you do.

_______ When the truth about your abuse from your dad came out, no one believed you. To keep peace in the family you went back to pretending nothing was wrong.

_______ Your mom gets sick and she needs around the clock care. No one is able to fill this need but you. But the catch is that you have to go to her house to do it, since she would feel better being in her own home. Your dad will be there too and you will have to sleep in your old bedroom. After several phone calls from your mom, you give in and go "for her sake" out of guilt.

______ The family calls to come to Christmas at your house. You remind them that everyone is welcome to come, except your dad. If they want him to be there at Christmas, then you will be happy to send the gifts and wish them all a wonderful holiday.

______ Your sister wants to meet you at your dad's house for a family weekend. Although she is angry at your stand not to come, she respects you because you are firm but kind.

______ The truth was told about your abuse by your father and several of the family members, that you love, turn against you. You feel sorry that they are in denial, but continue with your life, shaken but determined.

______ Your mom gets sick and it is determined that you are the designated caregiver. She calls you numerous times and is sounding very pitiful trying to convince you to come to her house during the illness. You firmly but kindly remind her that SHE is welcome at your house at any time but your father is not. You will help her if she is willing to honor your decision and your family. Her guilt trips soon end and she chooses to pay a caregiver.

Dear Lord, Please help me to establish right boundaries in my life by…

In Jesus' Name, Amen.

REMINDER: Remember to Journal daily…

1. (http://www.selfgrowth.com/articles/Baker4.html; taken from an article by Barbara Baker)
2. *Do Rejection Fears Rule Your Life?* by Royane Real
    http://www.selfgrowth.com/articles/do_rejection_fears_rule_your_life.html

Chapter 10

The Necessity of Forgiveness

Who I Am In Christ

Read daily. Put your name in the blank.

The Word of God Says...

___________________ is the light of the world...Matthew 5:14

___________________ is part of the true vine...John 15:5

___________________ is Christ's friend...John 15:15

___________________ is a joint heir with Christ...Romans 8:17

___________________ is righteous and holy...Ephesians 4:24

___________________ is a child of light and not of darkness...1 Thessalonians. 5:5

___________________ is an enemy of the devil...1 Peter 5:8

___________________ is a slave of righteousness...Romans 6:18

___________________ is enslaved to God...Romans 6:22

___________________ is born of God, and the evil one - the devil - cannot touch me.
      1 John 5:18

Objective:

- To learn what forgiveness is and what it is not
- To understand that no healing can take place without forgiveness of the offender
- To understand that no healing can take place without forgiveness of yourself
- To understand how to forgive

Inspiration:

Isaiah 35:1-10 (AMP) 1) THE WILDERNESS and the dry land shall be glad; the desert shall rejoice and blossom like the rose and the autumn crocus. 2) It shall blossom abundantly and rejoice even with joy and singing. The glory of Lebanon shall be given to it, the excellency of [Mount] Carmel and [the plain] of Sharon. They shall see the glory of the Lord, the majesty and splendor and excellency of our God. 3) Strengthen the weak hands and make firm the feeble and tottering knees. [Hebrews 12:12.] 4) Say to those who are of a fearful and hasty heart, Be strong, fear not! Behold, your God will come with vengeance; with the recompense of God He will come and save you. 5) Then the eyes of the blind shall be opened, and the ears of the deaf shall be unstopped. 6) Then shall the lame man leap like a hart, and the tongue of the dumb shall sing for joy. For waters shall break forth in the wilderness and streams in the desert. [Matthew. 11:5.] 7) And the burning sand and the mirage shall become a pool, and the thirsty ground springs of water; in the haunt of jackals, where they lay resting, shall be grass with reeds and rushes. 8) And a highway shall be there, and a way; and it shall be called the Holy Way. The unclean shall not pass over it, but it shall be for the redeemed; the wayfaring men, yes, the simple ones and fools, shall not err in it and lose their way. 9) No lion shall be there, nor shall any ravenous beast come up on it; they shall not be found there. But the redeemed shall walk on it. 10) And the ransomed of the Lord shall return and come to Zion with singing, and everlasting joy shall be upon their heads; they shall obtain joy and gladness, and sorrow and sighing shall flee away.

The Journey Continues…

What is Forgiveness?

The most crucial area of healing for the sexual abuse survivor is forgiveness. The pain of violation, being misused, not being believed or worse, being accused, can close the door to forgiveness in the heart. The first step in the process of forgiveness begins with recognizing there is resentment, therefore there is a need to forgive. The second step in forgiveness is to recognize who the enemy is that has caused the pain. But, God never asks us to do what He has not done.

Over and over the words, "I already forgave." or "There is nothing to forgive." are used as a means of denial. The reality of forgiveness is much deeper than most of us can comprehend, much less actually live up to. According to the Bible, forgive (sah-lahch), means to pardon; spare someone; to relieve someone of the burden of their offense.

What most of us do in the act of forgiveness is to say we are sorry in order to relieve the negative feelings we feel toward the person, but we no longer want to be in relationship or in even the same location as the offender. "I forgave them, but I still don't like them."

The next type of forgiveness is one where forgiveness is granted to the person but the relationship is never the same as before. The person is no longer trusted, suspiciousness keeps everyone involved on edge, but the original offense can be claimed as forgiven and "let go of".

The final type of forgiveness is the one that the Bible refers to, and is the one that God the Father gave to us through the death of His Son, Jesus Christ. This is the "sah-lahch" forgiveness we are asked to imitate as Christians. We are to actually admit that there was an offense, then relieve the offender of the burden of their guilt, even though responsibility is never denied. This forgiveness is a total forgiveness from the heart where all negative feelings for the offender are ended and the relationship is fully restored. This does not always include a physical restoration of relationship, but means a restoration of relationship where the desire to ruin their reputation through sharing what they have done is gone, and good will for their future is focused upon.

Often when I come home from shopping, I arrive at my home in a hurry to unload my car. In an effort to not make a second trip to the car, I load my arms as full as I can get them, which more often than not, are too full. My desire then becomes a desire for help and relief from someone who is willing to come to my rescue, and take some of my load upon them. How thankful I am when I once again have the freedom of movement with no fear of dropping anything, hurting myself, or not being able to open the door to my house. I have been rescued from my bad decision to overestimate my ability, mercy is given to me, and restoration of my true ability is returned. All of this forgiveness for my actions are given by someone who could have made the decision to look out the window and refuse to become actively involved in my dilemma; after all, it was my decision to make a poor choice in the first place. This is a simple example, but one that we can all understand because we all do it. We get ourselves in dilemmas and ask people to help get us out of them.

1.) Look up and write out Luke 23:34.

2.) Do you believe that you could forgive the person or people who wounded you as well as unconditionally love them?

3.) **Read Luke 23:35-48.** Who were the people mocking Jesus?

Who were the people that Jesus gave His life for?

If you have accepted Jesus as your Lord and Savior, did He die on that day for you also?

By now, you have also realized that Jesus died for all, the ones who hung Him on the cross, the ones who cast lots for His clothing, His own people, you, and the person who abused you. Forgiveness is for all from Jesus, no matter the sin and no matter the cost.

Forgiving Others

Here is a story about Corrie ten Boom. She was in her 40's during WWII and knew that she would face prison if she were discovered helping Jews. One day a man came to her and asked her for money to help a Jewish woman escape. She gave him the money. The man was a Nazi agent and had her set up. She, her sister, and their aged father were sent to prison and eventually wound up in a concentration camp. Corrie was the one family member that survived the internment.

At one point she and her sister were forced to stand naked waiting for a shower while a Nazi guard looked them over. Corrie felt great anger against the man. When her sister died, the anger grew. But God was with her. She was miraculously released at the end of the war and allowed to return home.

After a while, the Lord specifically led her to begin ministering to former Nazis. She was very good at this work and her loving nature resulted in many coming to know the Lord.

While she was speaking one day, a Nazi soldier from her former concentration camp came towards her after her talk. She was overcome with anger and wanted nothing to do with him. The man extended his hand to shake her hand and relayed the fact that he was now a Christian. He asked her to forgive him.

Corrie knew that it would be impossible for her to forgive him without God's help. She said an immediate prayer asking God to help her forgive him and give her the ability to shake his hand. She relays that a sudden rush came through her as she, in an act of obedience, raised her hand to his, the warmth of God's love flowed through her. It was very difficult, but with God's help, she grew greatly in the Lord that day.

In giving our emotions to the Lord, His love and forgiveness can come through our hearts to others. It's amazing what God can do with our worst emotions. Ask Him for help. He is faithful.

What do the following scriptures tell you about forgiving others?

Romans 14:10

Mark 11:25

Matthew 18:21-22

Forgiveness is not optional!

Forgiving doesn't necessarily bring physical restoration of a relationship. It is likely that the relationship with the perpetrator will not be restored. Your relationship with your family may not be immediately restored. Sometimes relatives must let go of their own bitterness, apart from you. You are not responsible for anyone's emotions but your own. Forgiving is an act of the will and impacts one's intimate relationship with God. The act of forgiving is not optional as relayed by Jesus in His sample prayer, which we refer to as the Lord's Prayer:

"Forgive us our debts, as we also have forgiven our debtors. For if you forgive men when they sin against you, your heavenly Father will also forgive you. But if you so not forgive men their sins, your Father will not forgive your sins." Matthew 6:12, 14-15 (NKJV)

Forgiving Others When They Don't Deserve It

Another example of forgiveness is from the Old Testament. Joseph was the son of Jacob, a wealthy Israelite. During Joseph's life there are clear examples of being forsaken by his brothers and sold into slavery, falsely accused by Potiphar's wife who tried to seduce him and when he refused her, she lied about him. He was then forgotten in prison in spite of promises made by people he helped saying they would help him get free. Finally, he was favored by Pharaoh and became ruler over all of Egypt under Pharaoh.

Joseph's story begins in Genesis 37 and ends at Genesis 46. This is very good reading if you care to read through it, but for the sake of time, we will cover only the high points.

4.) **Read Genesis 37:3-4.**

How did Israel (Jacob) feel about Joseph and how did his brothers feel toward him?

Read Genesis 37:8. Joseph dreamed that he would someday rule over all of his family. How did the brothers feel toward him now?

Read Genesis 37:25-28. Joseph has been kidnapped and sold into slavery by his own brothers. You have, by your abuser, been taken and treated however they chose to treat you with no control of your outcome at the time. Can you relate to what Joseph is feeling? Explain your answer.

During Joseph's slavery in Egypt he was sold to Potiphar who gave him charge over his entire house. During this time Joseph was sexually assaulted by Potiphar's wife. Because of his loyalty to his master and fear of God, he refused her advances, running away from her. In his haste to leave her, she was able to grab his coat and strip him of it, leaving proof that he was actually in her presence. The wife took revenge on Joseph by lying to her husband and falsely accused Joseph of assaulting her. The result of this was Joseph being imprisoned for the next 20 years.

5.) How many years or months has it been since your sexual abuse started or occurred?

6.) You may believe you were imprisoned for all of that time for a crime you never committed and tried to avoid. What have you done to begin the process of opening those prison doors and being set free?

Eventually, Joseph was released from prison and was set in charge of all of Egypt, second only to Pharaoh, because he had favor with God. During this time a great famine occurred throughout all of the land, causing his brothers to come to Egypt to purchase grain for their families for food. Because of the separation between Joseph and his family, he had changed in appearance and was not recognized by them. But, he recognized them.

7.) **Read Genesis 42:9.**

What was the first thing that Joseph did when he saw his brothers?

What was the second thing he did?

8.) A natural human response to a traumatic event, or to the people involved, is to first try to forget. But, at times, something will occur that will bring memories screaming back into your mind. What is your first response at those times? For example: run away, strike out, turn a cold shoulder.

In spite of the events that took place with his brothers, Joseph missed his family and wanted to be reconciled with them. Testing and tricking them, he was able to force them to bring his only full brother, Benjamin, to Egypt.

9.) **Read Gen 43:29-31**. What was Joseph's reaction to seeing his little brother, whom he loved?

10.) Is there someone in your abusive past who knew nothing about the abuse occurring, yet you want to be in relationship with this person even though it causes you to be around the abuser? Who is it?

The moment of truth had finally arrived for Joseph. **Read Genesis 45:1-9.**

11.) Emotions can be very strong when self-protection is involved. What does verse 1 and 2 say happened with Joseph's emotions?

Everyone in the palace heard or heard about Joseph's sobbing. The news spread quickly. Because he was second only to Pharaoh and had saved all of Egypt, he was now family to and loved by Pharaoh and the Egyptians. Joseph knew that the first reaction that his new family would have to his biological family would not be favorable once they learned of his past and what they had done to him.

12.) What did Joseph do in verse 1 to protect his family's reputation?

In many instances of sexual abuse, the victim is compelled to keep the secret for the sake of the family. This can cause resentment and a sense that the members of the family have more value than the one who was abused. This is especially true if the abuser is treated as though they are not guilty of any crime.

13.) Why do you think that Joseph chose to protect his brothers' reputations?

14.) What was Joseph's abusers' first reaction to his statement in verse 3?

15.) Have you confronted your abuser or others for the abuse? If so, what was their reaction to you? If more room is needed, please continue writing in your journal at the end of the chapter.

16.) What has their reaction made you aware of?

17.) Reread verses 4-8. Do you believe that Joseph is speaking out of denial and excuses about what his brothers did, just so he can be a part of the family once again?

Consider Joseph's position in Egypt. Joseph is a leader, accustomed to being in charge of people. He knows he is an authority figure. In verse 4, Joseph says for them to come closer to him so no one else can hear him speak. Softly he said "I am your brother Joseph, whom you sold into Egypt." No one else knows the ten brothers sold one into slavery. It is Joseph's closely guarded secret. He is well aware that if Pharaoh hears of the crime his brothers had committed against him, he could punish them severely. But, Joseph also needed to tell his brothers who he was, so he revealed the long held secret.

The main reason that Joseph had been willing to accept his brothers back into his good favor was that he had already forgiven them. It had been over 20 years, and Joseph had to learn to forgive many wrong actions against him in his life. The most important one was to forgive his family.

18.) Do you have a member of your family or a friend that you need to forgive? (Not necessarily a sexual abuse issue.)

Forgiveness is not an option. Anger will never leave until we learn to love in spite of being wronged. Being able to love the sinner but hate the sin can be a monumental task, but it can be accomplished. Joseph did not like what had been done to him, but he also realized that the events in his life happened with a greater plan in mind. What was important was that he was able to achieve great honor through humility and a willingness to let go of the past. Not that he was sacrificed in order to save his family.

19.) What did Joseph tell his brothers to do in verse 5?

20.) Was Joseph in control of the situation that he was in now with his family?

21.) Did Joseph secretly want to punish his brothers for their actions?

22.) Have you ever told someone that you forgave them, when secretly you still hadn't forgiven them?

If so, now is a good opportunity to ask God to forgive you of your sin of un-forgiveness and let go of the bitterness that is stored up inside of you.

Dear Lord, Forgive me for…….

In Jesus Name, Amen.

　Caught in the Act of Grace Women's Bible Study

Forgiveness of an Offender

1 Corinthians 5:1-6 (AMP) *"1) IT IS actually reported that there is sexual immorality among you, impurity of a sort that is condemned and does not occur even among the heathen; for a man has [his own] father's wife. 2) And you are proud and arrogant! And you ought rather to mourn (bow in sorrow and in shame) until the person who has done this [shameful] thing is removed from your fellowship and your midst! 3) As for my attitude, though I am absent [from you] in body, I am present in spirit, and I have already decided and passed judgment, as if actually present, 4) In the name of the Lord Jesus Christ, on the man who has committed such a deed. When you and my own spirit are met together with the power of our Lord Jesus, 5) You are to deliver this man over to Satan [a]for physical discipline [to destroy carnal lusts which prompted him to incest], that [his] spirit may [yet] be saved in the day of the Lord Jesus. 6) [About the condition of your church] your boasting is not good [indeed, it is most unseemly and entirely out of place]. Do you not know that [just] a little leaven will ferment the whole lump [of dough]?"*

23.) In stark contrast to Joseph hiding what his family did, Paul is telling the Corinthian church to publicly expose this man's sin. What is the difference in the two? See verses 2 and 6 for the answer.

24.) What is the desired end result of dealing with this scandalous incest in verse 5?

2 Corinthians 2:5-11 (AMP) *5) "But if someone [the one among you who committed incest] has caused [all this] grief and pain, he has caused it not to me, but in some measure, not to put it too severely, [he has distressed] all of you. 6) For such a one this censure by the majority [which he has received is] sufficient [punishment]. 7) So [instead of further rebuke, now] you should rather turn and [graciously] forgive and comfort and encourage [him], to keep him from being overwhelmed by excessive sorrow and despair. 8) I therefore beg you to reinstate him in your affections and assure him of your love for him; 9) For this was my purpose in writing you, to test your attitude and see if you would stand the test, whether you are obedient and altogether agreeable [to following my orders] in everything. 10) If you forgive anyone anything, I too forgive that one; and what I have forgiven, if I have forgiven anything, has been for your sakes in the presence [and with the approval] of Christ (the Messiah), 11) To keep Satan from getting the advantage over us; for we are not ignorant of his wiles and intentions."*

25.) Here is another situation within the church in Corinth. This time the person who has committed incest has a different reaction to being caught. What is that reaction? See verse 7.

26.) Why is Paul telling the people to forgive this person and "reinstate him in your affections and assure him of your love for him" in verse 8?

27.) Are the people who have been wounded a concern for Paul in verses 9-10?

28.) In verse 11, Paul suggests that Satan can get the advantage over us if we are not careful. In this situation, what does it take to keep Satan from filling the people with bitterness and resentment?

29.) When he is speaking to the people, he is including the abuser in keeping bitterness and resentment away from them all. Have you ever been humbly apologetic for something you did, but the other person involved refused to forgive or forget? What did you do when forgiveness was refused?

It is easy to forgive someone who apologizes, but rarely does a sexual abuse victim get an apology from the abuser. The purpose in forgiving the abuser is not to let him/her off the hook or to live in denial of the action. The purpose is to let yourself stop being angry and having to fight off resentment in every area of your life. A little yeast spreads through the whole lump of dough. A little bitterness spreads through your whole life.

Why Must We Forgive?

Now is the time to give the gift of forgiveness, even though the person to whom you are giving this precious gift does not deserve it. Use the following journal page to write a letter to the offender giving forgiveness.

30.) **Read Job 42:10**. What was given to Job when he prayed for his friends?

Restoration comes to us when we are willing to forgive the very people who offended us. It is not necessarily for their sake, but for ours. Un-forgiveness is a bitter root. When it takes hold of you and grows, your whole world will become ugly and hurtful.

31.) Name the bitter roots (offenses) from your past, i.e. Divorce or ex-spouse, parents, siblings or abuser who may have caused you great pain; a friend who did you dirty or someone who stole something from you. Slowly think of things from your recent past or long-term past that causes you to have mixed feelings when you think about them. Each of those things are a root of bitterness that need to be pulled out of you.

a.)

b.)

c.)

d.)

e.)

f.)

g.)

Write on the back page if more things come to mind. Do this part slowly and give it much thought. Rage or complete anger is not necessarily a part of a bitter root. It is the little foxes that spoil the vine and it is the little offenses that cause us to have grievances with most people.

32.) Now that you have thought of the offenses and the names of the people or a description of them (if you only remember an event and not a name), write a letter to each of those people in your journal. It does not need to be long. Name the event or offense, then forgive the person and then ask them to forgive you. Leave these letters in your journal, do not mail them. Bring your journal to the next class and be prepared to burn each letter. These letters are for your healing alone, not for others.

When we forgive someone of something and "let them off the hook", it is not for their sake as much as it is for ours. When we don't forgive of every offense that comes our way, it is like drinking poison and hoping the other person will die. They are able to go on with their lives and probably never realize that they have wounded you. You are the only one who carries the burden of the un-forgiveness with you. You are connected to them as long as you hang on to the pain that they have caused you. Release the pain and you will release yourself from unnecessary baggage.

Dear Lord, Thank you for helping me to …….

In Jesus' Name, Amen.

Goals that were accomplished during Caught in the Act of Grace Bible Study

- Learned how to feel again and know that life is going to have bumps in it but it is okay to feel those bumps and move past them.
- Gained insights by breaking isolation through sharing of stories.
- Learned biblical tools that can be incorporated into daily life.
- Learned how to use those tools.
- Discovered relationship and boundaries from a biblical perspective.
- Regained ownership of your own life and choices.
- The idea of an instant cure is no longer the desire.
- Know that sexual abuse does not identify who you are, but it does affect who you are.

Congratulations,

You have completed the Caught in the Act of Grace Bible Study. Through these past weeks you have had your share of tears, laughs, pain and realizations. The things about yourself and others that had confused you at times have now come into the light. You are more normal than you ever realized before!

When you began this study, there were probably many times you wondered what in the world you were doing. Your family and friends may have wondered the same thing. But now that you are at the end of the study and there is nothing more to do than to look forward to a changed life, go ahead, breathe a sigh of relief. What you anticipated your feelings may be at this point may have been realized, or they may not have been. You may have believed that the pain in your heart would be gone, and it is not. You may have wanted answers to have conclusions, and they may not. But I can assure you, this is just one step of many on a path before you that will last a lifetime. Just know that you are on the right path. The other steps in your path may not need an intense amount of attention, but remind yourself that you must still go forward.

Please remember that in the weeks and months ahead, you will have a "settling" in you that is necessary. Your heart and mind have been through a lot, now they need to rest and look back at the things you have learned. Use the information to help you continue forward when you are tempted to go backward. Never let your wounds return to you, but remind yourself that you have a scar that may be tender to touch, but is just a scar. Your past will never change; it is forever a part of who you are. But it was your past that made you who you are today, wonderfully and awesomely made.

If you will continue on this road to recovery of your past, you will succeed. Never look back with bitterness or anger, but look forward to the rewards of gracious life with God and people. Open your heart and allow the anxiety of the past to be replaced with a willingness to allow people to be themselves and to come and go in and out of your life. Pain is a part of love that we can never avoid but is healthy and necessary. Go ahead and live your life with freedom, forgiveness and joy.

God bless you and keep you. May His face shine upon you and give you peace.

Darla Weaver

Resource List

Post Abortion

Forgiven & Set Free: A Post Abortion Bible Study For Women by Linda Cochrane
www.christianbook.com or 1-800-CHRISTIAN

Acts of Grace Ministries Forgiven and Set Free Bible Study Leaders Guide.. www.actsofgrace.net

The Gift of You: Keepsake…www.angelsinheaven.org or (972) 424-5508

Beyond Regret: Entering Into Healing & Wholeness after an Abortion DVD
featuring Sydna Masse…www.Paracletepress.com or 1-800-451-5006

Her Choice to Heal: Finding Spiritual & Emotional Peace After Abortion
by Sydna Masse…www.christianbook.com or 1-800-CHRISTIAN

No One Told Me I Could Cry: A Teens Guide to Hope and Healing After Abortion
by Connie Nykiel…resourcecenter@family.org

Baby Doll: Suggested Lee Middleton Dolls … www.leemiddleton.com

Miscarriage and Stillbirth

Free to Grieve: Healing & Encouragement for Those Who Have Suffered Miscarriage and Stillbirth
by Maureen Ranke…www.christianbook.com or 1-800-CHRISTIAN

Sexual Abuse

Caught in the Act of Grace Bible Study for Women by Darla Weaver… www.actsofgrace.net

Acts of Grace Ministries, Caught In the Act of Grace Bible Study Leaders Guide for Women

Caught in the Act of Grace Bible Study for Men by Darla Weaver ….. www.actsofgrace.net

Acts of Grace Ministries, Caught In the Act of Grace Bible Study Leaders Guide for Men

When Trust is Lost: Healing For Victims of Sexual Abuse (Booklet)…
Free from RBC Ministries (donation suggested) www.rbc.org or (616) 972-2210

General

Father's Love Letter DVD…www.christianbook.com, 1-800-CHRISTIAN, or
www.fathersloveletter.com

Darla Weaver Testimony DVD …www.actsofgrace.net

Total Forgiveness by R.T. Kendall ….. www.Amazon.com

Commentary on The Whole Bible by Matthew Henry

Made in the USA
Monee, IL
30 July 2020